Music publishing, copyright and piracy in Victorian England

Music Publishing, Copyright and Piracy in Victorian England

A twenty-five year chronicle, 1881–1906, from the pages of the Musical Opinion & Music Trade Review *and other English music journals of the period*

GATHERED BY

James Coover

Mansell Publishing Limited
LONDON AND NEW YORK

First published 1985 by Mansell Publishing Limited
(A subsidiary of The H. W. Wilson Company)
6 All Saints Street, London N1 9RL, England
950 University Avenue, Bronx, New York 10452, U.S.A.

British Library Cataloguing in Publication Data

Music publishing, copyright and piracy in
Victorian England: a twenty-five year chronicle,
1881–1906 from the pages of the Musical opinion
& music trade review and other English music
journals of the period.
1. Music printing—History
2. Publishers and publishing—Great Britain—
History
I. Coover, James II. Musical opinion & music
trade review
070.5′794′0941 ML112

ISBN 0-7201-1749-6

Library of Congress Cataloging in Publication Data

Music publishing, copyright, and piracy in Victorian
England.
Bibliography: p. 145
Includes index.
1. Music—Publishing—England—Sources. 2. Copyright—
Music—England—Sources. 3. Music—England—19th
century—History and criticism—Sources. 4. Music—
England—20th century—History and criticism—Sources.
5. Music and society—Sources. I. Coover, James,
1925–
ML286.9.M87 1985 070.5′794′0942 84–27317
ISBN 0–7201–1749–6

Typeset by J & L Composition, Filey, North Yorkshire.
Printed in Great Britain at the University Press, Cambridge

Contents

For
Philip Lieson Miller

For many of us who have not
had a chance to say it before:
Thanks, for letting us—as you phrased it—
'spread our wings'. We have tried to live up to
your trust.

Introduction

For twenty-five years, the music publishers in Britain warred with those who copied music illegally and struggled with a Government irresolute about helping to suppress those crimes. That is the central theme of this *Chronicle*.[1] Running parallel throughout are other colourful strands of human enterprise and controversy: the reciprocal mistrusts and sometimes open dislike between musicsellers and publishers; the determination of those publishers to protect a *status quo* against all persuasions; the guile and arrogance of the pirates, and the curious group which made excuses for their piracy; the proliferation of protective associations put together by publishers, retailers, and even the pirates, and the sub-division of those into other alliances; the galling difficulties caused by a legislative mechanism that would not seem to work; the complex, almost byzantine, methods adopted by the publishers to achieve some satisfactions in the courts; the apparent indifference of the public to most of these events, and in reverse, the publishers' indifference to the public's interests (in all of which, composers occupied an unfortunate middle ground!); the persistent effects of the infamous Harry Wall's earlier activities on the formulation and application of copyright laws; the enmity aroused by a traditional system of pricing music to wholesalers, professionals, retailers, schools and public—a system displeasing to just about everyone; the constant threats posed by sections of copyright legislation proposed and passed in America and Canada and at the Berne Convention; the attempts to establish the French system of *petits droits* and a British counterpart of the Société des Auteurs, Compositeurs et Éditeurs de Musique; finally, the growing insolence of the pirates and ruthlessness of the raiders which generated dozens of small scuffles and appearances before magistrates.

Touched on, in passing, are printing practices and costs in both Britain and abroad; auction sales of engraved and stereotyped music plates and copyrights; various views of the 'royalty' system; the workings of Parliament; an ill-fated catalogue of British music in print; and of course, musical taste.

For piracy to profit, it had to fulfill a demand, and at the turn of the century, the public's desire for sheet music seemed unlimited.

1. *This travail is noted briefly by Ronald Pearsall in his* Edwardian Popular Music *(Newton Abbott: David & Charles [c1975]), pp. 97–100, 'The Music Pirates', and summarized by Percy Scholes from the pages of the* Musical Times *in his* The Mirror of Music, 1844–1944 *(London: Novello & Co., 1947), pp. 744–45.*

The British music hall was at its zenith, popularizing dozens of new songs every week, and cheap pianos, one of the better fruits of the Industrial Revolution, were being purchased in the tens of thousands for middle-class homes. The number of persons playing musical instruments was immensely greater than a few decades earlier, and there was little distraction, as yet, from the gramophone, none from the 'wireless'. Music at home was live music, and the music-makers wanted a big selection. The pirates—at first tentatively as though to test the legal waters—began to supply 'the songs of the day, the songs of the hour' in tawdry lithographs, but nevertheless at very affordable prices. When the impotence of the British copyright protections became apparent, and as demand for the product increased, so too did the pirates, in number and brazenness. Piracy of music touched the lives of more people than did the pirating of books, for the illegal copies were hawked aggressively in the streets and marketplaces of almost every city and town in the British Isles. The buying public did not care that the merchandise was illegal and scruffy. The notes were the same, and the prices were low. Abroad, British copyrights were reproduced without permission or payment in America, Australia and Canada for a similarly delighted public.

Composers' pocketbooks were seriously hurt, some fatally. Publishers' profits dwindled, in a few cases to the point of bankruptcy. Though neither Parliament nor the publishers seemed to care, small, retail musicsellers also lost heavily. (Curiously, the dealers' more frequent and more strident complaints were addressed to their treatment by the publishers, not to the pirates' larcenies!) Wounds were inflicted on the pirates and on members of the publishers' gangs in raids on the pirates' 'lairs', but to judge by the sources used for this *Chronicle*, none serious.

Piracy was a furtive business, and how it was done never has been fully documented. It was not, for the most part, a cottage industry. In the big cities especially, it was a complex business operation run by a 'mastermind' planner who contracted with and managed printers, agents, runners, and warehousemen—who often did not know each others' names. At the end of the process the material reached the salesman, the street hawker. This unfortunate individual, part of the group most exposed to arrest, was time and again referred to in court as a 'person of no known address'.

The enemy of the members of this group, the other central character in this story, was the Music Publishers' Association. It was formed in 1881, but not, at the outset, to combat piracy. As the turn of the century approached, however, piratical activities and the passage of legislation to suppress them became overriding concerns—costly concerns. The Association's actions against the pirates, in the streets and in the courts, and its struggles with

Parliament for relief crescendo up to 1906 and the passage of the curative Copyright Act.

That act, which ended piracy of copyrights, came just in the nick of time, for almost immediately, the publishers were compelled to turn the full force of their organizations, treasuries, legal advisors, and their friendships in the Parliament to the problems of performing rights, problems arising principally from the growth of the gramophone industry. It was well, therefore, to have one sticky wicket, the suppression of illegal reprints, taken care of.

'History does not disclose its alternatives', and we are left to guess how much different the course of music history might have been had the pirates not flourished. I have made no great attempt to pry those alternatives out of this *Chronicle*. It is simply a summary of reports appearing in the *Musical Opinion and Music Trade Review* from 1881 to 1906 with additions, here and there, from other journals and documents when it seemed necessary to embellish the *MO&MTR* accounts, to cover events not fully reported there, or to reassert the importance of certain events. I have tried to intrude into the story as little as possible, letting it unfold as it would have to a steady reader in this era, with a minimum of footnotes and explanations. Confusions or contradictions raised in one report from the sources are usually clarified in succeeding ones, and if not drastic, I have let most of these stand. That is the way it was. On the legal side, many of the assertions reported, especially those concerning laws, are over-simplifications, but to explain each of these would, again, be an intrusion. In most cases they do not grievously misinform the reader, and most are put to right elsewhere in the narrative.

Most of the addenda come from the *London and Provincial Music Trades Review* (*L&PMTR*), because of its similarities to the *MO&MTR*, because it was issued side by side for many years, and because it was aimed at the same audience. To avoid laying my own interpretation on the situations reported in both of these, I have retained as much as possible the style of the prose and have quoted extensively from them and other sources. Of course, the selection process itself is an act of interpretation, and the reports chosen are those which seemed to me most noteworthy. What the editors of the *MO&MTR* and others elected to report, in what sequence, at what length, and where those accounts were placed in the journals tell us something about what was on the minds of the principal readers, the music publishers, and I hope to have reflected that accurately in the selections.

This *Chronicle* could have begun almost anywhere in the century

—at 1842, for example, with the passage of a copyright act whose proscriptions and spirit continued to effect events throughout the period up to 1906. The *Chronicle*'s closing date also could have been moved, perhaps further along to the passage of the Copyright Act of 1911, or that of 1914 (and the establishment of the Performing Right Society). But I have chosen to start with the founding of the Music Publishers' Association, an organization at the nub of most activites and discussions concerned with publishing, copyright and piracy—then and now. The minutes of its meetings and the texts of its notices, circulars and memorials to the Government provide a chronicle in themselves.

I have stopped the story at the end of the turbulence created by the pirates. The period leading up to the Copyright Act of 1906 which quelled that disturbance, was a time of growing agitation, depression and, yes, strained relations among those affected by the illegal trade. This *Chronicle* itself rises to a frenzy just before the Act is passed, depicting honestly, I hope, the increasing amount of space being given to the problems in all of the journals and newspapers, and the increasingly hysterical tone of voice in much of the reporting. Even anger! Immediately after passage, there is an almost instantaneous deflation (the metaphor of a punctured balloon is apt)—a time of unrestrained relief, joy and unnatural camaraderie among all concerned. For a brief time, the only enemy is the pirate, and he is in retreat. It is the way a good tale ought to end.

A WORD ABOUT SOURCES

The principal source for this narrative, the *Musical Opinion and Music Trade Review* (*MO&MTR*), first appeared on 8 October 1877. Without the trade review section, it is still being published. Accounts from it have been supplemented and complemented by those from other journals of the period, especially the *London & Provincial Music Trades Review* (*L&PMTR*), which began in the same year, 1877. It is remarkable that the two journals, very much alike in almost all ways, prospered equally for so many years. The *MO&MTR* carried the trade review section until 1964; the *L&PMTR*, with its name changed to *Music Trades Review*, continued after 1916.

A typical monthly issue of either journal during the period of this narrative would probably include most of the following:

1. a section of news about concerts and recitals by Ysaÿe, Patti, or other artists during the preceding month; a review of the opera season to date or of noteworthy festival performances;

2. a few reviews of newly published music (usually serious music);
3. a signed, lengthy (2–3 page) article on, e.g., 'Current freights for Pianos, Organs, &c.', on copyright law, or on 'Street Music';
4. what were called 'Leaders'—small articles, perhaps half a page in length, about such things as 'Stamps on hire contracts', a new exhibition, 'A new Copyright Bill', important auctions of musical interest;
5. a gazette listing new legislation affecting the trade;
6. one part of a continuing article about an exhibition, the manufacture of a certain kind of piano, voicing organs, or on copyright;
7. a section of trade notes from abroad;
8. a department answering legal questions or printing verbatim portions of laws or recent judicial decisions;
9. obituaries;
10. several pages of brief notes about the publishing or instrument manufacturing industry;
11. a page or two devoted to trade in the provinces;
12. a register of new patents issued and their abridgements;
13. and throughout, advertisements for music, pianos, organs, banjos, harmoniums, wood, tools, auctions, and sundry gadgets.

Most of the other British music journals of the period have also been examined thoroughly (see Bibliography). When they are mentioned in the narrative, their titles are given in full, not abbreviated. In most of them, articles and notices about events and personalities in the music trade appeared so infrequently that it was tempting to include everything they had to say. I have not.

In addition to the *MO&MTR* and the *L&PMTR*, principal sources included several unica preserved in libraries and archives, chief among them, the *Minute Book* of the Music Publishers' Association in London (shortened to *Min. Bk.* throughout). The Association and its Secretary, Mr. Peter Dadswell, graciously allowed me to study this record of the MPA's meetings. Though there are some records missing (none in the *Min. Bk.* date earlier than 1884), it is a cache of information which would repay study by others interested in this field—and particularly beyond 1906 when this *Chronicle* stops. Mr. Oliver Neighbour, head of the Music Library at the British Library, also made available to me Arthur Preston's *Clipping Book* and the four volume set of *Pirated Music* (both described briefly here in note 176 at December 1905) which Preston must have carried with him while, as an agent for the MPA, he prosecuted hawkers and pirates in various courts all over the British Isles.

Practically everyone involved in this tale was very busy issuing notices, memorials, manifestos, circulars, warnings, and signs—the publishers, the pirates, members of Parliament, musicsellers' organizations, the Chamber of Commerce, the Police, Customs, and others. A quick glance at the Appendix called 'Missing Documents' will show that I have been unable to find many of these in their original state. That they existed (and may be in one of the hundreds of archives I could not search), there is no doubt, for they are noted and often quoted in one or several of the sources used for this story. I am very grateful again to Mr. Dadswell of the MPA, to several publishers (among them Chappell Music, Ricordi of London, Stainer & Bell, and Schott, London), to the British Copyright Council and the British Copyright Protective Association, Ltd., and others for trying to find copies of these notices.

I had hoped to embellish this publication with at least one contemporary photo or drawing of a street hawker selling sheet music, but none has been found despite the generous efforts of a number of organizations, including the BBC Hulton Picture Library, the Greenwich Public Library, and the Museum of London (Ms. Lindsey Fulcher, Librarian). A prolonged search in person and by mail of dozens of London print shops was also unproductive. Even a search by Mr. Colin Mabberley, Curator, through the extraordinarily rich Mander and Mitchenson Theatre Collection in Sydenham proved fruitless. I am grateful to one and all for their efforts.

A second Appendix was originally planned. It would have contained all of the texts of the pertinent copyright laws in effect between 1881 and 1906, and copies of them were obtained. The idea was abandoned, however, because most are already available in Strong's *Dramatic and Musical Law* (see Bibliography). Though the book is not widely available, it appears from time to time in the antiquarian book market, and a number of libraries own it. The full text of the Copyright Act of 1906 does appear at the appropriate place in this narrative, for its merciful passage, after all, culminates our story.

Literature cited in this chronicle is included in the Bibliography along with a few books for background reading selected from an almost limitless number. I have assumed that musicians/readers will already be familiar with many of the standard works on music printing, publishing, copyright, and on British music history. Rather than cite dozens of informative works on the fascinating subject of the British music hall, I have, instead, listed Senelick's superb bibliography.

Legal citations for many pieces of legislation and court cases referred to in the narrative are included in notes in order to particularize the legislation or trial discussed. Those citations are also provided in the separate lists of Statutes and Cases (under those rubrics) in the Index. In some instances it has been impossible to provide exact citations, so vague was a journal's account of an event or a document. For helping me with this aspect of the work, for leading me to, if not through, some of the mysteries of legal bibliography—and for much useful advice—I thank Joan White, Ellen Gibson, and Marcia Zubrow of the Law Library at the State University of New York in Buffalo, and Ms. Stephanie Kenna in the Official Publications Library in the British Library.

I am also grateful to the Research Foundation of the State University of New York and to the American Council of Learned Societies for grants-in-aid which helped in the completion of this and several other studies of the British music trade in the nineteenth century.

The Chronicle

Dramatis Personae

The events chronicled here involve many persons. Most appear on stage briefly, the brevity of their appearance belying, in numerous cases, their importance. A few dominate the action, influencing the proceedings dramatically, and they receive repeated notice from the reporters of the time. They are the principals of our story.

Ashdown
One of a number of English families engaged in music publishing during the period covered by this chronicle. (See also here, BOOSEY, CHAPPELL, DAY, FRANCIS, and NOVELLO.) EDWIN Ashdown (1826–1912) and Henry John Parry, who had been managers of the distinguished publishing house of Wessel, took over the business and formed the company Ashdown & Parry on Wessel's retirement in 1860. Ashdown became sole proprietor when Parry retired in 1882. From 1883 to 1970, when the business ceased, its premises were in Hanover Square. EDWIN served as President of the Music Publishers' Association (the MPA) in 1901. Two of his sons, PERCY and FRANK, were members of the firm. FRANK, manager of the Canadian branch, was also, at one time, manager of the Anglo-Canadian MPA, Ltd., which maintained offices in both London and Toronto. PERCY was U.S. representative of the firm and opened a New York City branch in 1891.

Balfour
Two brothers, ARTHUR JAMES (1848–1930) and GERALD WILLIAM Balfour (1853–1945), played significant rôles in the struggle to establish strong copyright protection for music publications while members of H.M. Government. ARTHUR JAMES, later the first earl of Balfour, authored a small tract, *Economic Notes on Insular Free Trade*, the piracy of which probably spurred him to help the music publishers' cause (see note for May 1905). During the years of this chronicle he was Prime Minister and First Lord of the Treasury. His brother, GERALD WILLIAM (the second earl), an M.P. for Leeds, held a variety of governmental posts including that of private secretary to his brother. From 1900 to 1905 he was President of the Board of Trade which considered, in a number of meetings, the problems of music copyright.

Balfour, Alexander Hugh Bruce
The sixth Lord Balfour of Burleigh (no relation to the preceding) was an M.P. from 1876 to 1921 and Parliamentary Secretary to the Board of Trade from 1888 to 1892, in which year he enters this story by suggesting a 'short bill' to protect copyrights.

Boosey
A prominent music publishing and instrument manufacturing firm whose ownership has remained in the family through many generations (and about which far too little is known). The business was begun by THOMAS B. about 1795. On his retirement in 1816, the music part of it went to his son, another THOMAS, who continued with his sons, CHARLES and JOHN, until they inherited the firm. JOHN, in turn, drew his nephews, WILLIAM and ARTHUR, into the work. Not all stayed with Boosey & Co. WILLIAM left to join Chappell & Co. in 1894 (see separate entry below). He was the only Boosey in the limelight during the war against the pirates chronicled here, though the firm was a charter member of the MPA. Various family members attended meetings of that Association throughout this era, including ARTHUR, C. T., and GEORGE Boosey.

ARTHUR was also the firm's representative to the Musical Defence League in 1905. (His brother WILLIAM's *Fifty Years of Music* (1931), has little to say about the family members excepting JOHN. Besides him, only ARTHUR and C. T., William's elder cousin, are even noted.)

Boosey, William
Adopted by his uncle, John Boosey, of the firm Boosey & Co., WILLIAM entered the business at the age of sixteen in 1880. He left it in 1894 to take the post of Managing Director at Chappell & Co. Chappell published thousands of popular musical works and may have suffered more than any other publisher from piracy. The fiery WILLIAM was a leader throughout the long campaign against the illegal printers, their friends in Parliament (see here, CALDWELL), unjust American and Canadian laws and practices, and the French system of *petits droits*. He was President/Chairman of the MPA from 1902 through the passage of the new Copyright Act of 1906.

Caldwell, James
M.P. for Glasgow and a rich calico manufacturer. He was friendly to the pirates' cause and battled against all copyright legislation desired by the music publishers from about 1903 until the passage of the new Act in 1906. His widely distributed 'Memorandum' (sometimes called 'Manifesto') offered his objections to the elements of the various bills which had been introduced. It was strongly rebutted, point by point, by the redoubtable William BOOSEY (see July 1904).

Chappell
A music publishing family (not all of whose members are mentioned in this chronicle). The firm was established in 1810 when SAMUEL, with John Baptist Cramer and Francis Tatton Latour, bought the well-known publishing business of Goulding, D'Almaine & Co. On SAMUEL's death in 1834, his sons, THOMAS PATEY (1819–1902) and WILLIAM (1809–1888), took over the management, assisted by a third son, SAMUEL ARTHUR (1834–1904). THOMAS, who entered the business at fifteen years of age, became senior partner in 1845 and served as Director for almost sixty years. He was a close friend of Sir Arthur Sullivan, one of the original directors of the Royal College of Music, and a governor of Royal Albert Hall. It was he who called the first meeting of a group of music publishers to establish the MPA. He was elected its first President in 1881, serving until 1901. The other brother, WILLIAM, left the firm amicably in 1843 to join the firm of Cramer, Beale and Chappell, from which he retired in 1861. He was best known for his work with the Musical Antiquarian Society and for his publications, one of the more familiar, his collection, *Popular Music of Olden Time*. SAMUEL ARTHUR, who with THOMAS founded St. James Hall and the Monday 'Pops', left Chappell & Co. in 1880.

EDWARD Chappell, a grandson of the founder and a junior partner, persuaded William BOOSEY (q.v.) to become its Managing Director in 1894. Another grandson, FRANK, was a partner in the music publishing firm of Metzler & Co. (which George T. Metzler had inherited from his father, Valentine). On Metzler's death in 1879, FRANK became sole owner and was one of the first members of the MPA.

Clayton, Henry Reginald
A barrister, an authority on copyright, and by 1898 a partner in the firm of Novello, Ewer & Co. He was Chairman of the Music Trades Section of the London Chamber of Commerce during the anxious years of this chronicle and testified repeatedly before various governmental committees about the need for stronger copyright protections. 'A certain brusqueness of manner, due to an isolated temperament, was a misleading index to his nature', according to his obituary in the *Musical Times*, January 1933.

Cutler, Edward, Q.C.
The author of the important *Manual of Musical Copyright Law* (1905), an excellent amateur musician and composer, and at one time Grand Organist of the Freemasons. Like CLAYTON (q.v.), Cutler testified about copyright problems at numerous hearings conducted by Departmental Committees of Parliament.

Day, David George

Day (1850–1929) began his publishing career with the firm of Hopwood & Crew in 1865, later formed a partnership with James and William FRANCIS (q.v.), who were then working at Chappell & Co., and founded the firm which later became Francis, Day & Hunter. Day was the active partner. Both his sons, FREDERICK and CHARLES, and those of his partners, worked in the business. He joined the war against the pirates early and was one of their more combative opponents—in word and deed. Some of his firm's agents were accused several times in court of assaults on hawkers. He organized the Musical Copyright Association (President in 1902), as well as the Musical Defence League of the MPA. He lent one of his employees, John Abbott (author of *The Story of Francis, Day & Hunter*, 1952) to the Copyright Association to be its Secretary. From about 1900 to the passage of the new Act of 1906, Abbott and George PRESTON (q.v.), chief agent of the MPA, managed to forcefully seize millions of illegal copies from the pirates and their hawkers. The *MO&MTR* commented in November 1897 about David Day: he was 'the mildest mannered man that ever cut the throat (so to speak) or scuttled the ship of the piratical song printer'.

Dixey, George

Was Secretary of the Music Publishers' Association from 1885 to 1912 when he was succeeded by his son, C.J., who served from 1913 to 1945.

Fisher, James

This was the alias of Frederick WILLETTS, 'King of the Pirates' (q.v.). According to Willetts, the name was given him by his associates because he had previously been in the fish business. When he brazenly formed a limited company of pirates—capitalized at £1,000—it was called James Fisher & Co. (Ltd.).

Francis, Day & Hunter

One of the more active music publishers in the war on the pirates under the leadership of David DAY (q.v.). It was founded in 1877 as W. & J. Francis & Day, later changing names when Harry Hunter joined the partnership. It was very much a family affair involving the brothers WILLIAM and JAMES Francis, DAVID and FREDERICK Day, and several of their sons. Harry Hunter sold out his interest in 1900. One of the firm's most notable acts was the introduction of 'Sixpenny Music' (see Index).

Monkswell, Robert Collier

Second Baron Monkswell (1845–1909) supported the publishers in their attempts to achieve better copyright protection and was responsible for the introduction of numerous pieces of legislation for that purpose. He was M.P. for Bury St. Edmunds, member of the London Chamber of Commerce from 1889 to 1907, and Lord-in-Waiting to H.M. Queen Victoria from 1892 to 1895.

Moul, Alfred

Composer and journalist, attended the first meeting of the MPA in July of 1881, remaining friendly with the music publishers until 1889 when suits brought by the Société des Auteurs, Compositeurs et Éditeurs de Musique, which he represented in the British Isles, brought him into conflict with William BOOSEY (q.v.) and others. The threat to the publishers inherent in the 'retrospective clause' of the Berne Convention, and to whose use the Société was allied, was not eliminated until a decision was reached in the landmark case of Moul *vs.* Groenings in 1891. Moul later won a suit for libel against William Boosey in 1903, Boosey unwisely having likened Moul's practices to those of Harry WALL (q.v.). In another rôle, Moul had been Manager of the famous Alhambra Theatre in Leicester Square from 1894 to 1898 when he stepped down, presumably to devote full time to the activities of the Société. Asked to resume control of the theatre in 1902, he did so, but nothing more is heard of him in this chronicle.

Novello

Novello & Co. was a family business initiated in 1811 with the first of a series of publications authored by VINCENT Novello (1781–1861). It became a full-grown music publishing house in 1829 under his eldest son, JOSEPH ALFRED Novello (1810–1896) and Henry

Littleton. It issued vast numbers of musical works (by 1893 there were 450 employees and 29,000 titles in its catalogue) as well as the journals *Musical World* (begun in 1836) and the *Musical Times* (begun in 1844). In the latter was printed the MPA's ambitious but ill-fated 'Catalogue of All Music Published in Great Britain'. Littleton took over the management when JOSEPH ALFRED retired in 1856, later adding the catalogue and name of Ewer & Co. ALFRED L. Novello succeeded Littleton in 1887. A charter member of the MPA and one of the most active in the struggle to secure better copyright laws, the firm began and paid for the 'friendly' case, Novello *vs.* Ditson, in the U.S. courts, which tested the legality of the 'manufacture clause' in the U.S. Copyright Act of 1891.

O'Connor, T. P.
'Tay Pay' (Thomas Power, 1848–1929) was 'England's leading journalist and nationalist member of Parliament for the Scotland Division of Liverpool' (*MO&MTR*, August 1906). He enters the action of this chronicle in 1905, working closely with William BOOSEY (q.v.) and others to defeat the protractions of James CALDWELL (q.v.) and almost single-handedly managed to move a private bill to passage as the new Copyright Act of 1906, which dealt a death blow to piracy. For these efforts he was honoured at a complimentary dinner in November of 1906.

Preston, George Arthur
Preston (1870–1926) was chief agent of the MPA for the prosecution of printers and vendors of piracies. He came from the staff of BOOSEY & Co. (q.v.). With John Abbott from the staff of FRANCIS, DAY & HUNTER (q.v.), he travelled throughout Britain to seize illegal copies and to press cases in court. A collection of about 250 pieces of pirated sheet music gathered for his use in those prosecutions, and a volume of newspaper clippings which he assembled during this time, are in the British Library (see May 1905 and December 1905, note number 176).

Wall, Harry
Almost always referred to by his contemporaries as 'the infamous', he was the (probably self-appointed) representative of something called The Copyright and Performing Rights Protective Society. He managed quietly to gather assignments of copyright to a number of works frequently used by performers, especially at penny readings and benefits. As representative of the Society he would then, it is said, 'pounce' on those innocents who were unaware that the performing rights were reserved. No list of these rights was ever made public; only by paying Wall an exorbitant fee could a performer or theatre manager know what was assigned to Wall. By law, until the Copyright (Musical Compositions) Act of 1882 was passed (called the 'Walls Act'), magistrates were required to exact damages of 40 shillings from each of Wall's unlucky victims. In 1887 he was sentenced to jail for representing himself as a solicitor—though not so qualified. When William BOOSEY (q.v.) likened Alfred MOUL's activities (q.v.) to those of Wall, Moul sued for libel and won the case in 1903.

Willetts, James Frederick
Flamboyant, self-styled 'King of the Pirates', who operated in London, was the central character in the 'Great Conspiracy Case', which marked the beginning of the end for organized piracy—and for him. By the time he had finished the sentence handed down in this case, the new Copyright Act of 1906 effectively deterred any renewal of such operations. He was known by a number of names—'Fisher', 'Mr. W.', 'The Colonel', and as James FISHER (q.v.), the name he attached to the limited company of pirates which he formed. He was also Secretary of what he called the Peoples' Music Publishing Co. (Ltd.), designed—according to him—to bring music cheaply to the masses and award composers more generous compensation than that offered them by the existing music publishers.

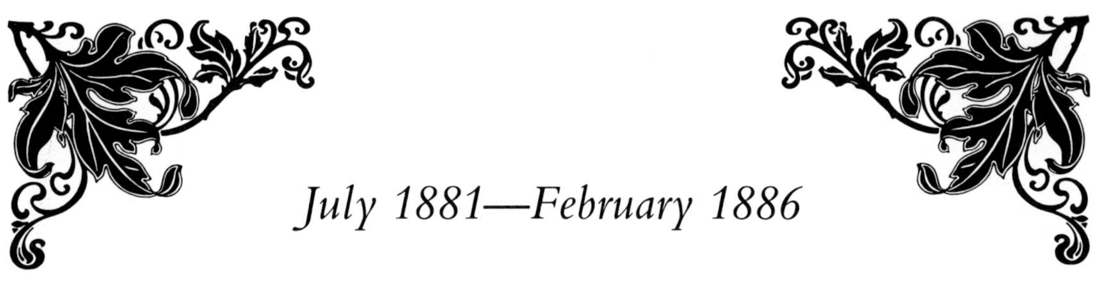

July 1881—February 1886

The Music Publishers' Association is formed.

Meadows White reviews music copyright laws and performing rights.

The Copyright Act of 1882 solves some problems, chiefly those created earlier by the infamous Harry Wall.

Boosey wins a case against Townsend, loses some others.

A Song Folio—*the ubiquitous* Song Folio—*arrives and the publishers wonder if H.M. Customs is doing its job.*

A Catalogue *comes and goes.*

American copyright laws and behaviour meet with disapproval.

Nervousness about the provisions of the Berne Convention surfaces.

A first notice goes to musicsellers warning them about piracies, but doubts are voiced about who should be warning whom about whom.

Boosey has bad luck with Stanford's Savanarola—*twice.*

The Anglo-Canadian Music Publishers' Association is introduced.

Publishers' pricing practices draw complaints from both musicsellers and the MO&MTR, *but they go unanswered.*

July 1881

At a meeting in early June called by Mr. Thomas Chappell, a group of London music publishers resolves to establish the Music Publishers' Association. Charter members include Boosey & Co., Chappell & Co., Metzler & Co., Novello, Ewer & Co., Cramer & Co., R. Cocks & Co., Schott & Co., Enoch & Co., Ashdown & Parry, Augener & Co., Jefferys & Co., B. Williams & Co., Hutchings & Romer, J. Williams & Co., Stanley Lucas, Weber & Co., J. Blockley, Hopwood & Co., and E. Chappell.[1] A subsequent meeting fixes the annual membership fee at two guineas,[2] elects Thomas Chappell Chairman, Mr. Ashdown Treasurer. Stanley Lucas volunteers to serve as Secretary. A motion is passed to send out a circular inviting all music publishers to join.

On 10 June, at Metzlers', Mr. Chappell reviews the reasons for forming the association. Attending this meeting—in addition to the charter members—are Lamborn Cock, J. George Patey, E. A. Willis, J. McDowell, and others. To frame a constitution for the organization, a committee is elected unanimously consisting of Thomas Chappell, John Chappell, Emile Enoch, Mr. Augener, Mr. Hutchings, Stroud Cocks, G. F. Jefferys, and Mr. Patey. This constitution is presented later at the 1 July meeting. Among its 12 points, number 2 sets out some objectives of the Association: to protect the interests of the music publishing trade, especially in the proposed new Copyright Act and in the matter of performing rights; to try to settle disputes among members by arbitration; to consider the best means for winding up insolvent estates.[3]

MO&MTR, p. 358

The editor of the *MO&MTR* comments that the Association 'intends to look on hard work with a light heart' and commends the establishment of the organization.

The first instalment of a lengthy article on 'Copyright with regard to the Works of Musicians' appears. It is a transcript of a paper read by F. Meadows White to the Musical Association in which he discusses salient provisions of the prevailing Copyright Act of 1842,[4] beginning with the strong protection afforded manuscript and unpublished works by common law: 'The author or owner of any literary composition or work of art has a right, so long as it remains unpublished, to prevent the publication of any copy of it by any other person.' This applies even though, in the case of a dramatic work or a musical composition, the piece has been publicly performed. Neither common law nor the Copyright Act, however, protect a work originally published in a foreign country. The

1. *The Music Publishers' Association* Minute Book (see *Introduction*) *contains no official minutes of this 'private gathering', only a clipping of the article from the* MO&MTR! *Added to it in manuscript, however, are the names of authors and composers who were there, including: F. C. Burnand, Clifton Bingham, Sutherland Edwards, W. S. Gilbert, George Grossmith, B. C. Stevenson, F. E. Weatherley, Luigi Arditi, Frederick Cowen, Odoardo Barri, Tito Mattei, C. V. Stanford, Paolo Tosti, and Miss Hope Temple. A private committee was set up consisting of three authors, three composers, and three publishers, with Mr. Alfred Moul, who later grows at odds with the Association, as its Secretary. (See Dec. 1888 entry here.)*

2. *A manuscript correction of the printed rules in the* Minute Book *alters this to five guineas.*

3. *During the years covered by this chronicle, 1881—1906, however, the Association never did discuss 'insolvent estates'—at least there is no record of such in the minutes of its meetings!*

4. *5. & 6. Vict., ch. 45, 1 July 1842.*

distinction between common law and statutory protection is emphasized and the provisions of the Act are discussed, the first, an interpretation clause which includes 'sheet of music' in the protection afforded a 'book'. Meadows White notes that this interpretation was applied by the courts in numerous cases prior to the 1842 Act—by Lord Mansfield in a case brought by John Christian Bach claiming copyright for one of his sonatas, and in the cases Storace vs. Longman and Clementi vs. Golding.

Musical compositions for the stage are protected by law under the expression 'dramatic piece'. Piano arrangements of operas, new accompaniments and symphonies to old airs in which there is no copyright are similarly guarded. 'Publishing' has been defined carefully as exposing a work for sale or offering it gratuitously to the general public. The Act, applying to the United Kingdom and all colonies, settlements, dominions, and possessions of the Crown, regulates reprinting and importations. An important provision interprets the recognizable paraphrasing of an air or melody forming part of an opera as an infringement of the copyright on the opera as a whole; Meadows White cites the case of D'Almaine vs. Boosey over Auber's *Lestocq*, one of whose melodies Musard had arranged as a waltz and Boosey had published.

How copies are reproduced and whether or not they are distributed for gain does not alter the protection afforded the owner; the gratuitous distribution of copies of Benedict's *The Wreath* to members of a Philharmonic Society was deemed an infringement in Novello vs. Sudlow. Meadows White describes other points relating to copyright: those eligible to acquire or hold a copyright; the prohibition against acquiring copyright of a work published earlier out of the U.K.; copyright as personal property; the inheritability of copyright; how copyright may be assigned by registry at Stationer's Hall; and the differences between 'division' of copyright, 'share' copyright, and 'licenses'.

The writer also notes the difficulty of distinguishing 'fair use' of quoted sentences, phrases, or paragraphs from a book from 'fair use' of portions of a musical creation; 'no equivalent has been found for the "inverted comma" of literature.' *MO&MTR*, pp. 359–62

August 1881

Meadows White, in the second part of his paper, ends a discussion of performing rights with examples showing how the law has worked to protect owners of those rights. He next describes several amendments to the Copyright Act which the Copyright Commissioners have recommended, the most interesting perhaps, that which would change the expiration date on a composer's works, no matter when written or published, to thirty years after his or her death, and in the case of works published after death, thirty years after deposit of the work in the British Museum.

In a lengthy and lively discussion following the presentation, Mr. Littleton worries that the cost of registration and re-registration mandated by the proposed new bill would be prohibitively expensive. He notes the frequent sales of copyrights at auctions and elsewhere in which sometimes hundreds of small works change hands;[5] he contrasts that with sales of book ownership which involve many more plates to a set but fewer titles, all to be registered at the same price as sheets of music.

Mr. Ashdown states that the interests of the composer and publisher are identical and 'presumes' that Meadows White has not read the new bill which is in charge of Mr. Hastings of the Law Amendment Society and which has already been read a second time.

Mr. W. H. Cummings[6] is concerned about protecting the 'whole right' in various performances and fears, as things are, a creation like the *Elijah* may be taken 'by the gentlemen in Hatton Garden and applied to the barrel-organ.' Meadows White responds that publisher and composer have the power now to prevent such a performance 'but no remedy for it'.

The day concludes with a long discussion of whether ownership of a copyright includes automatically the performing rights and the questions posed by compositions in which the composer owns the music, another person the words. *MO&MTR*, pp. 401–05

Elsewhere a Mr. Martin complains that all of the proceeds earned by a concert for the benefit of a parish church were swallowed up by a £4 fine for infringement of performing rights to a song by Balfe. He suggests that all copyright music be distinctly labelled with a warning, 'Not to be performed in public without permission'.

A Mr. Bevan presents the composer's side of the case along with his regrets that a charitable concert went for naught. He notes the recent formation in Britain of the International Musical, Dramatic and Literary Association which will function as exclusive representative of 'La Société des Auteurs, Compositeurs, et Éditeurs de Musique de France'. *MO&MTR*, pp. 406–07

Those attending the 1 July meeting of the Music Publishers' Association accept the new constitution. Some discussion follows about recruiting others and about the implementation of Rule 10, but a resolution to delete the rule is defeated. *MO&MTR*, p. 417

A brief paragraph notes an announcement about a 'copyright register' existing at 93a Regent Street which can be searched by

5. *In the years covered by this chronicle, a single London auction firm, Puttick & Simpson, conducted sales of copyrights and plates for over 100 consignors, almost all publishers, whose names appeared in the catalogues, and for twenty-six others whose names did not.*

While these were predominantly sales of lightweight, popular works, the sheer number of the sales indicate dramatically the liveliness of the music trade. Even during the later years of this chronicle, 1900—1906, when music publishers spoke dolefully of a business dangerously depressed by the pirates, action in Puttick's sale room remained brisk and highly competitive, and some of the publishers offering the gloomiest public statements about the state of their business were the fiercest contestants in the bidding for properties to add to their catalogues—many of them works which had been repeatedly pirated! (See also *note 168 at May 1905.)*

Chappell, Ashdown, Novello, Hopwood & Crew, Francis, Day & Hunter, Boosey, and several others—leaders in the fight with the pirates—were not selling many of their copyrights but were very busy buying those consigned for sale by Weber, Pitt & Hatzfeld, Mathias & Strickland, Patey & Willis, Phillips & Oliver, Orpheus, Lyric, Adams, Beal, and numerous smaller firms.

These sales and the transfer of copyright and plate ownership in the nineteenth and twentieth centuries are the subject of a forthcoming essay by this writer in a celebration volume in honor of Richard S. Hill.

6. *Cummings was Professor at the Royal Academy of Music, possesor of a distinguished private music library, and author a few years earlier of an important article, 'The Formation of a National Music Library',* Proceedings of the Musical Association, *4(1877): 13–26.*

performers to find 'protected' songs on payment of a 5s fee.
MO&MTR, p. 420

September 1881

'From 1800 to 1881, the firm of Ricordi have published 47,000 musical works by 2,500 different authors. They possess 4,500 MS. scores by Italian and other composers. In 1880 [alone!] they struck off 50,000 pages of music.' *MO&MTR*, p. 457

October 1881

J. A. Westwood Oliver takes the side of Mr. Martin [Sept. 1881] and criticizes Mr. Bevan's response. As part of his argument he notes that whoever pays the price of a book purchases also the right to read it and asks why the price of a song should not include the right to perform it. He hopes the Association Mr. Bevan mentioned will better the understanding between composers and performers and supports strongly the printing of a warning on each piece of music which requires permission to perform.
MO&MTR, p. 19

November 1881

The addenda to Mr. Meadows White's paper on copyright read at the seventh session of the Musical Association [see July 1881] is reprinted from the Association's *Transactions* along with an editorial calling attention to the fact that one provision of the proposed bill would satisfy both Mr. Martin and Mr. Westwood Oliver [October 1881]: Unless a printed notice appears on a piece (published after the law becomes effective) indicating that the performance rights are reserved, along with the name and address of the owner of those rights, the right to perform would be automatically a part of the purchase.[7] *MO&MTR*, pp. 48, 57–58

April 1882

A lengthy 'Special Report' of the 7 March 'special general' meeting of the Music Publishers' Association is featured. About twenty publishers attend. Thomas Chappell, in the chair, tells newcomers what the organization has been doing, primarily in getting the copyright bill altered. He notes that the bill did not pass and awaits the next session. A solicitor for the Association has drafted two forms for the members, one for assignments, another covering royalties—royalties, i.e., to be paid to singers by publishers. It limits the term that the song is the performer's property and prescribes the number of times it must be publicly performed.[8] Another circular, 'To the Music Trade', is presented [signed by the same twenty firms in attendance] announcing two new rules: 1) 'All collectors purchasing music for cash will be supplied with a

7. *The bill enacted, the Copyright (Musical Compositions) Act of 1882, was necessitated principally by the actions of Mr. Harry Wall and was, in fact, termed 'The Walls Act'. This arrant gentleman, a supposed representative of something called the Copyright and Performing Right Protection Society, began a series of legal proceedings against a number of singers, many of them amateurs, most of them performing at penny readings or charitable entertainments. Because some of the pieces they performed bore no notice that performing rights were reserved to the Society, the victims were unconscious of the danger from a Society about which they were unaware. Wall pounced, and they were forced by the courts to pay a penalty of 40s. for each 'infringement'. (That penalty was fixed by law at 40s. until 1888 when the Copyright Act passed that year granted courts some discretion on the size of such fines.) To combat Wall, the Act of 1882 required owners wishing to reserve performance rights to print such a notice on each copy of a piece. The law, unfortunately, had no retrospective force.*

That Wall has the law on his side is conceded by the Musical Times *in June 1881, but it disapproves of his methods and, to warn the 'unsuspecting', begins publishing lists of compositions 'protected' by the Society (pp. 295–96).*

The organist William Spark described his encounter with Harry Wall in an amusing section, 'How I Once Spent Christmas Eve', pp. 341–47 of his Musical Memories *(new ed., rev. and corr., London: W. Reeves [1896?]).*

8. *No copies of the original found. (See 'Missing Documents', Appendix, pp. 143–4)*

receipt . . .'; 2) 'collectors obtaining music upon credit will be served only when their orders are entered in the proper collecting book of the house which they represent . . .'[9]

Mr. Boosey moves a resolution that publishers will close accounts with all provincial dealers who, because they receive music on better terms than the London wholesalers, re-sell music to those businesses. Unanimously carried. *MO&MTR*, pp. 277–78

9. *As above.*

May 1882

In an article about 'The House of Ricordi', the writer notes that 'every year 40,000 plates are engraved and the number of these plates reaches today over 600,000. From 8,000 to 10,000 are melted again every year . . . The catalogue published in 1875 is a . . . volume of 738 pages'. *MO&MTR*, p. 325

June 1882

In a case heard in the Chancery division on 6 May, Chappell & Co., the plaintiff, seeks and is granted an injunction restraining the defendant, Messrs. Boosey and his agents from performing in public a piece copyrighted by Chappell. The judge notes that the Copyright Act confers two rights on the owner—the right of producing it in book form and the sole liberty of performing it in public. Boosey contends that the purchaser of the printed work purchases the performing rights automatically. The judge does not concur. *MO&MTR*, p. 369

December 1882

The Secretary of the Music Publishers' Association asks the *MO&MTR* to warn its readers that any copying of a copyrighted song, even by hand, is an infringement.[10] He notes that advertisements appearing in journals 'circulating primarily among ladies' offer to provide such copies. The Association has recently begun proceedings against one lady and has threatened 'another in respect of this offence'. *MO&MTR*, p. 115

10. *The same warning appears in the* L&PMTR, *15 July 1888 (p. 19) and the* Musical Times, *1 Dec. 1892. An editorial comment about the problem in* The Times, *1 Jan. 1893 (p. 16) includes notice of 'an invention expressly intended for amateurs to copy printed music'. See also here 15 Jan. and March 1888, and 15 Sept. 1890.*

The Minute Book *contains no minutes for this year, but those for a meeting ten years later, on 29 April 1892, report a lengthy discussion about the problem under the heading 'Girl's Own Paper'.*

February 1883

The *MO&MTR* exults over the decision of the Circuit Court in Boston which has granted Novello an *ex parte* injunction, stopping performances of Gounod's *Redemption.* The article, 'An Act of American Justice', bemoans the fact that a book published in England can be re-published by someone in America (and vice-versa) without the authors receiving a farthing. England would agree to a copyright treaty to solve this tomorrow if America were willing, but America is not. 'The balance of exchange is all in her favour'.[11]

'Meanness, we think, can hardly go farther, or sink deeper', than in the recent reprint and performance of Gounod's work in

11. *cf.* Musical Times *report, here under August 1883.*

America. As soon as the English pianoforte score appeared it was reprinted, one edition even imitating exactly the appearance of the English book and stating that it was 'Novello's edition'. Novello managed to stop that, but then performances began with an orchestral score concocted from the published pianoforte score.

The Court's decision should establish the principle that publication of a pianoforte score does not authorize another composer to write an orchestral accompaniment, misrepresent the composer, deceive the public with a 'maimed' composition, and cheat both publisher and composer out of their rightful profits.[12]

MO&MTR, pp. 75–76

12. *Another favourable, though not final, court decision in this case is reported in the 1 December 1882* Musical Times, *that of Novello vs. C. G. Röder of Leipzig, the firm responsible for printing an edition of Gounod's work for an American publisher, and against the firm of Hofmeister for having ordered the reprinting. The Superior Court in Leipzig supports the plaintiff, Novello.*

The Music Publishers' Association says it intends to compile and publish a 'Catalogue of all Music Published in Great Britain' (copyright and non-copyright) and asks publishers to assist by sending in their complete catalogue. *MO&MTR*, p. 218

March 1883

At its 30 January meeting, the Music Publishers' Association discusses a comment appearing in the *Family Herald* and apparently addressed to schoolgirls: 'It is certainly not illegal to copy printed music . . .' noting that copyists—some who transpose—advertise all the time. It is resolved to let the Association's solicitor see what can be done.[13]

13. *See note 10 at Dec. 1882.*

The 'Catalogue' [see above] is discussed at length, whether it should be issued monthly, in parts, and how complete it should be. Depositing copies of all publications with the Association's Secretary is proposed, and several members remark on the benefits that a German musicseller derives from their catalogue [Hofmeister?]. The Chairman thinks the catalogue will 'afford valuable information some forty-two years hence. That would not, however, be a very important question at the present moment'.

MO&MTR, pp. 258–59

April 1883

Novello & Co. have offered to print the quarterly catalogue of the Association in the *Musical Times* free of expense.

MO&MTR, p. 305

At the 12 March meeting of the Association the 'Catalogue' is the centre of attention.[14] Resolved, that the catalogue forms for February and March be sent to publishers forthwith, that the publication of the catalogue for the first quarter of 1883 be done as soon as possible, and that '2000 sheets of "notice of copyright to her

14. *Because the minutes of the MPA meetings preserved in the* Minute Book *do not commence until 7 July 1884, the earliest discussions of the 'Catalogue' are lost to us.*

Majesty's customs"[15] be stereotyped, and 1500 of them bound in fifteen books'.

The Secretary, at a committee meeting on 27 March, indicates that all parts of this resolution have been carried out. He is instructed by the membership to send out the forms for April–June and to have fair copy of the first quarter's catalogue ready for the printer by 16 April. *MO&MTR*, p. 308

15. *One of the 'Missing Documents', Appendix, pp. 143–4.*

1 July 1883

A note about the 'royalty system' comments on publishers' efforts to persuade professional vocalists to help promote songs 'for a consideration'. In a song sent by a publisher to a singer of the writer's acquaintance, a circular sets out a graduated scale of payments to be made if the song is sung in public, as well as other inducements, such as the announcement that 'the composer would be most happy to accompany the song at London engagements'. The fee varies according to 'the class of concert and popularity of the vocalist', and to collect, the performer is directed to send to the publisher a copy of the programme with the piece described as 'New Song', followed by the name and address of the publisher. Payment will be made within three months.[16]

Musical Times, p. 376

16. *F.J. Crowest was only one voice among many decrying this arrangement. In his* Phases of Musical England, *p. 153 ([London: 1881]), he railed about the 'system', calling it 'an abominable invention'. Allied to it was what Crowest called 'the signature business', which he also saw as a 'sore evil', the procedure by which, for a price, a popular artist allowed the publisher to print on each copy a phrase such as 'Sung by ——— ——— to great applause', along with a rubber stamp of the singer's signature.*

1 August 1883

'Copyright with America' discusses issues reported earlier in the February *MO&MTR*. The court's decision in the Gounod *Redemption* case has renewed the agitation of Eastern U.S. music publishers for an international copyright treaty. They will not be satisfied, however, with that which suits France and Germany; it must be one-sided. Every book affected by copyright must be printed and bound in America and issued within three months of its publication in England.

A long article, quoted from the *Boston Musical Record*, insists that 'opposition to the passage of an international copyright law comes from England'. The editor fancies that the whole article will have English readers rubbing their eyes at 'this curious case of topsy-turvey'.

Firms in the Eastern U.S. have long made a practice of publishing English works almost simultaneously with their issue in England, enjoying thereby a monopoly of supply for a limited time. They have paid British firms for this privilege, and the informal arrangement has been advantageous for all. Two or three years ago 'the great West' entered the picture. Not so scrupulous firms in Chicago and other towns in the region now flood the country with issues of English works at prices which drive the Eastern firms out of the market.

It will be seen, therefore, that in agitating for an international copyright law the Eastern firms have not the slightest idea of being just and generous at any sacrifice to themselves. The United States is the 'land of rings', which, under the provisions of the proposed law could keep authors' profits down. *Musical Times*, pp. 437–38

January 1884

A committee of the Association is appointed to interview Mr. Anderson, M.P. for Glasgow, on the question of colonial copyrights.

The Secretary is directed to demand from Mr. Irving of Toronto, the plates of certain English copyright songs he has reprinted without permission.[17] *MO&MTR*, p. 190

17. *The difficulties with Mr. Irving are mentioned in the* Minute Book *for the first time in the meeting of 27 April 1885. Success in the case lodged against Irving in Toronto is not reported until the minutes for 29 June 1885.*

In its issue for this same month, the *Musical Times* is gratified to find that by the recent copyright act 'every new composition can be safely presumed to be public property unless the contrary is stated upon the title page'. The law is not retrospective, however, and the editor suggests adding a line to existing plates indicating restrictions on performance. 'It would be a boon to those still in ignorance of the law, and to the many who cannot discover to what works the law applies . . .'[18] *Musical Times*, 1 Jan. 1884, p. 19

18. *See note 7 at Nov. 1881.*

February 1884

The first 'Music Publishers' Association Catalogue of all Musical Compositions Published in Great Britain', this for the quarter ended 31 January 1884, appears on pp. 113–19 of the February *Musical Times*. It includes works from over thirty music publishers arranged by medium, then alphabetically by composer. Price and publisher for each work are indicated.[19]

19. *But the experiment is short-lived, appearing only four more times, the last in February 1885 for the quarter ended 31 December 1884. Total number of pages—thirty-seven.*

March 1884

A sub-committee of the Association comprised of Messrs. Ashdown, Boosey, and Enoch is directed to draft and distribute to musicsellers a circular[20] offering a reward of £10 to persons who give information leading to conviction of anyone selling American piracies. *MO&MTR*, p. 279

20. *No copies found. (See 'Missing Documents', Appendix, pp. 143–4).*

'Enquirer', a country musicseller complains about the publishers and their travellers selling cheap to schools and self-proclaimed 'professionals', while travellers force dealers to accept a 'glut of unsaleable rubbish'. *ibid.*

April 1884
Messrs. Boosey & Co. are plaintiffs in an infringement case against a Samuel Townsend for selling two copies of 'The Song Folio', printed by Roe Stevens' Music of Detroit, Michigan. It contains reprints of thirty-nine Boosey copyrights, seventy-one owned by other British publishers. The price separately for all would be about £11, while the *Song Folio* sells for 4s 6d. Though evidence is introduced and witnesses testify that Townsend, a journey-man coach painter, did not own a shop, brought back only a few copies of the work when he visited Detroit intending to give them to friends, sold only two of them, and never acted as a salesman, the bench declares an infringement of copyright, fines him £5 for each copy sold, double for Boosey's song, *It was a Dream*—or face jail for two months. One of the plaintiff's witnesses is asked on cross-examination if he saw an advertisement offering a reward for the name of an offender [cf. March 1884]. *MO&MTR*, p. 328

May 1884
Under the caption, 'American Piracies of English Copyright Music', are printed two exchanges of letters between Mr. Harris, Secretary of the Association, and the Postmaster General's Office, and between Harris and the Commissioners of Her Majesty's Customs. Initiating the first exchange, the Association asked the P.G. to receive a deputation from the organization.

19 Feb.: The P.G. wishes to know what the subject of the visit would be.

23 Feb.: Subject would be the importation of illegal American reprints, in particular the *Song Folio*, containing mostly pirated editions of English copyrights, and to suggest means of stopping such practices.

3 March: The matter is already under consideration; a deputation 'is hardly necessary'. Customs has stopped a number of illegal importations but has received very few notices of copyright; until recently those received did not include the *Song Folio*, but now it is included and some copies of it have been intercepted. It is difficult to detect every packet of contraband, but renewed instructions are being sent to all offices.

6 March: Since it is difficult to identify packets that may contain contraband, the Association suggests that *all* music from America be prohibited entry. Numerous collections like the *Song Folio* contain piratical reprints. At its own expense, the Association is willing to send an expert to the Post Office to assist officials in identifying American piracies.

1 April: The Department cannot prohibit *all* music from America, only those which are contraband reprints, the titles of which have already been furnished a P.O. by its related Customs House. Iden-

tifying contraband is difficult, but in the last four months nearly 200 copies of the *Song Folio* have been stopped.

MO&MTR, p. 373

The second exchange begins with a letter on 23 February asking the Commissioner of Customs to receive a deputation from the Music Publishers' Association to discuss imports of American piracies, especially the *Song Folio*.

29 Feb.: The Commissioners send a copy of a memorandum describing the department's practice in detaining copyright works. They will be happy to receive from the Association any written suggestions which they may be disposed to offer.

3 March: The Association suggests that *all* importations of music from America be prohibited; ninety per cent are piratical reprints for there is no demand whatsoever in England for reprints of English *non*-copyright works. The Association offers to send experts at their own expense, to help point out what are American piracies. It is regrettable that there is no hope of the Commissioners receiving a deputation.

19 March: Directions have been issued which will be a further means of preventing importations of the works in question. A copy is enclosed. *ibid.*

Fearing that many American piracies are being introduced into Britain by various American steamship personnel, the Association also writes to steamship companies travelling between England and America asking their assistance. *MO&MTR*, pp. 373–74

July 1884

A special report on the annual meeting of the MPA reprints, virtually verbatim, the discussions which began with a 'Report of the Committee':

The 'Catalogue', which is being published quarterly by Novello in the *Musical Times* is believed to be a great service and benefit. The success against Mr. Townsend in 'The Derby Case' (as it is being called) is noted [see April 1884]; it depended on information gotten in exchange for the £10 reward that the Association had proffered. Secretary Harris describes his correspondence with steamship companies, the Customs House and the Postmaster General and reports that, as a result, the importation of a number of works, including the *Song Folio* has been 'successfully stopped'.[21] 'The committee have reason to congratulate themselves ...' The gratitude of the Association is tendered Mr. Boosey for the trouble he has taken with the Derby Case.

21. *This elation was perhaps a bit premature, for at the MPA meeting in October of this same year, a resolution was passed directing the Secretary to communicate with customs agents at Birkenhead and Liverpool 'about the importation at those ports of American pirated reprints . . . and to offer to send a clerk to Liverpool to purchase copies required for evidence of sale'. (*Min. Bk.*) See further deliberations reported here, June 1886.*

President Chappell commends the cooperation of the Customs House and the Post Office and several times urges members to send lists of their valuable copyrights to the Customs House, with the date of expiration (though 'people do not like to give [that] date'). The authorites will send the lists to the colonies also, but that will not help the Canadian market, lost to the Association because the Canadian government successfully applied to the British government to let them import American copies, and the Canadians have not taken care of the English owners' rights. As a result of further discussion it is moved and passed that a memorial on the situation be sent to 'the proper person' to get the order in council rescinded.

The President asks for donations from those present because the Derby Case has 'pretty well swept our funds out'. Done.

MO&MTR, pp. 468–69

Elsewhere it is reported that 'The New American Copyright Act', presently receiving attention in the U.S. Congress, includes the following clauses [summarized]:

1. Any citizen of a foreign country complying with provisions of this act shall be granted copyright and, in dramatic works, full performing rights.

2. Such copyrights are to continue for a term of twenty-five years.

3. To expire on the death of the owner.

4. No copyright granted under these provisions will be extended beyond the twenty-five year term.

5. If any foreign country, by law, grants U.S. authors the same protection, 'the President of the U.S. shall make public proclamation thereof and . . .' citizens of that country will be granted reciprocal rights.

6. Citizens of any foreign country which does not will not enjoy such rights. *MO&MTR*, p. 474

Under the caption, 'Law Intelligence', appears a summary and reprinting of many of the documents in the case of Boosey & Co. vs. Franke over the rights of representation of the words to Dr. Villier Stanford's opera, *Savanarola*. *ibid.*

17 July 1884
[A circular from Dod & Langstaff for the publisher Joseph Williams contains what was, under the existing copyright laws, a somewhat hollow threat of 'legal proceedings'.]

TO MUSIC SELLERS AND OTHERS.

Caution.

It having come to the knowledge of Mr. Joseph Williams, of 24, Berners Street, London, that piratical copies of the undermentioned works, the copyright of which is vested in him, have been imported and sold by music sellers in different parts of the United Kingdom, notice is hereby given that legal proceedings will at once be instituted against any person or persons who shall sell or offer for sale any copies or arrangements of any of the said works other than those published by Mr. Joseph Williams.

DOD & LONGSTAFF,
16, Berners Street, London,
Solicitors for Mr. JOSEPH WILLIAMS.

Dated this 17th day of July, 1884.

J. BRISSON.
Pavane Favorite.

A. DURAND.
Air de Ballet.
Gai Printemps.
Kermesse.
Menuet de Bergame.
Nuit Etoilee.
Sous les Bois.

B. GODARD.
Je ne veux pas d'autres choses (*song*).
Embarquez-vous (*song*).
Chanson de Florian (*song*)
Minuet Andante and Gavotte, op. 16.
Kermesse.

L GREGH.
Les Bergers Watteau.
En Poste Galop.

V. JONCIERES.
Serénade Hongroise.

Joseph Wieniawski
Valse de Concert Op. 3
Deuxième Impromptu Op 34. &c

J. LEYBACH.
Fête de Bergers (for complete list see catalogue).

J. MASSENET.
Scenes Pittoresques (4th orchestral suite).
Air de Ballet (from ditto).
Entracte Sevillana (Don César)
Marie Magdelene (and all arrangements).
Nuit d'Espagne (*song*).
Zanetto (Serénade du passant) (*song*).
Roman D'Arlequin
A Colombine (*song*).

C. NEUSTEDT.
Carillon (for complete list see catalogue)

E. PALADILHE.
Havanaise (L'Isolena).
Cuban Hammock (*song*).

J. B. WEKERLIN.
Marche a six mains.

For other works see general catalogue.

Carl Reinecke (Sketches)
Haus musik Op 77. &c. &c.

[And at about the same time in 1884, the firm of Simrock in Bonn was including English-language warnings against piracy in many of its publications, this, in an edition of Brahms' *Sieben Lieder*, op. 95:]

NOTICE.

The copying for payment, of any song, (no matter in what number,) published by my Firm, is piracy according to the law, and punishable as such. I hereby give notice, that I shall prosecute any person who infringes my copyright.

N. SIMROCK.

September 1884

The Music Plate Engraver.

THERE is an evil 'neath the sun,
Indeed there is an awful one;
As you'll agree, before I'm done,
Or else I'm but a raver.
Then listen while I state the case;
Just look the matter in the face,
And tell me should we not erase
The music plate engraver.

For years without the least complaint,
I've kept my temper like a saint;
But now all red the moon I'll paint,
Of war these lines shall savour.
I've whet my pencil to a point;
I've thrown myself clear out of joint;
With coals of fire I will anoint
This music plate engraver.

For carlessness he takes the cake,
Indeed his life's a grand mistake;
A quarter note he'll often make
A little semiquaver.
The staff, he doesn't seem to see,
I write an A, he'll punch a B;
Then sends the proof-sheet back to me,
This music plate engraver.

He don't know how to read or spell
For E, he's sure to punch an L;
But life's too short his faults to tell,
And I begin to waver.
I'm glad that he's not standing by,
Lest I myself his trade might try;
For surely I could *punch an eye*
For music plate engraver.

THOS. P. CULIAR.

'Law Intelligence' reports on the case called Boosey & Co. vs. Stanford. Boosey wishes the court to expunge from the entry made at Stationers' Hall by Dr. Charles Villiers Stanford certain words relating to copyright in the libretto of *Savanarola*. Boosey had bought from Stanford the publishing copyright, reserving to him the rights of representation. Boosey also purchased the copyright in the libretto from Mr. A'Beckett, the writer, and now contends that the entry made by Stanford was too wide inasmuch as Boosey retains sole copyright in the words. The decision is to dismiss the motion with costs. *MO&MTR*, p. 563

April 1885

Among 'Trade Jottings' is found this report: 'At a recent attempted sale by Messrs. Puttick & Simpson of the copyright of Mr. C. V. Stanford's two operas, the *Canterbury Pilgrims* and *Savanarola*, an offer of £5 was made for the first-named work, and there were no bids at all for the second.[22] Messrs. Boosey, who paid £1200 apiece for the operas a year ago, observe in a circular they have issued that "they had evidently over estimated the commercial value of the music of the future".'[23] *MO&MTR*, p. 355

22. *Puttick's sale of 24 Feb. 1885*

23. *The complete text of the circular appears in the* L&PMTR *15 March 1885. (No copy of the original found. See 'Missing Documents', Appendix, pp. 143–4).*

The formation of the Anglo-Canadian Music Publishers' Association is announced, its principal objective the printing, publication, and sale of English copyrights in Canada.[24] Though the Canadian Copyright Act of 1875 protects the copyright owner printing and publishing in Canada from importations of American piracies of those works, Canada has taken advantage of the provisions of an Order in Council and, along with other dominions, allowed the importation of American or foreign reprints of English copyright works. The Act of 1875 also prohibits the Canadian publisher from reprinting such works without licence, but that provision has practically become a dead letter.

These and other injustices in the existing laws, as well as a plea for their alteration, are included in a petition 'urged by the deputation that waited upon Sir Charles Tupper [the High Commissioner for Canada] in December last'. *MO&MTR*, p. 356

24. *Additional details and a commentary are provided in the* L&PMTR, *15 March 1885 (p. 13). Minutes of the MPA meeting for 24 Feb. 1885 remark that the Chairman, Mr. Chappell, explained the new Association and passed out copies of its prospectus. (No copy of the original found. See 'Missing Documents', Appendix, pp. 143–4).*

June 1885

A Trade Jotting: 'The question of discounts on sheet music is sorely exercising the minds of musicsellers just now . . . The whole question of pricing of sheet music is of course arbitrary and senseless, but it is difficult to suggest a remedy off-hand. One or two firms have marked their prices at two shillings nett, "breaking the barrier of the 4s standard", but the public have to be reckoned with, and they dearly like "under half price".' *MO&MTR*, p. 458

July 1885

'A Traveller's Tale', includes a lament for travellers with sheet music and for musicsellers trying to make a profit from it. How can they profit, the traveller asks, with the competition of 'the stores', the linen-drapers, bankrupt stock sellers, and the publishers who supply the public at the same prices demanded of the dealer.[25] Musicsellers have begun 'to look on "paper" as a nuisance and are giving up that branch of the trade'. *MO&MTR*, p. 512

25. *'Sheet Music Trade in the Provinces' in* L&PMTR, *15 May 1895 (pp. 11, 13) discusses many of the same alarming situations.*

Under 'Trade Jottings' the editors ask: 'When will the publishers agree to sell their music at nett? The nominal price is unsatisfactory. Here in London four shilling pieces are down to one and four! In these days of invention and steam presses, 4s. is too much for a piece of music. They should be marked nett'.[26] That price can be varied depending upon the author's worth, of course; 'the attempts of Messrs. Smithini or Blunderbury should [not] be priced level with the songs of Sullivan or Pinsuti'.[27] *MO&MTR*, p. 514

26. *Letters from dealers in 'Trade Correspondence',* ibid., *15 June 1895 (p. 13) echo these demands. Crowest,* Phases, *pp. 148–49,* op. cit., *speaks bitterly about the practice.*

27. *The problem is brought before the MPA Committee meeting of 24 Nov. 1885 in a letter read by Mr. Chappell, but after discussion the Secretary is instructed to reply stating that 'the Association [can] not usefully interfere in the matter'! (*Min. Bk., *42–43).*

August 1885

Several reports of progress are heard at the annual meeting of the MPA, mostly to do with piracies. Two actions against Messrs. Strange & Co. of Toronto on behalf of Mr. Ashdown and Mr. J. Williams have resulted in Strange & Co. having to destroy all plates and copies of certain songs.[28] Another Canadian illegally reprinting English copyrights has been ordered to deliver up all plates and music in his possession. The firms of Boosey, Chappell, Cocks, Cramer, Brewer, and Hopwood & Crew, after a court case in Sydney, have received damages and a public apology from a Mr. Charles Wilson, who has also been required to deliver all illegal copies to the publishers' representative.[29]

Efforts to rescind the Order in Council relative to colonial copyright [see April 1885] have not been very successful but will continue.

The Committee has discontinued the publication of the Music Catalogue; the original purpose could not be fulfilled and 'it became useless'. *MO&MTR*, p. 563

28. *Referred to in the minutes of the MPA Sub-Committee meeting of 20 Oct. 1884 (*Min. Bk., *7–8); in the minutes of the Committee meeting for 23 Dec. 1884 (*Min. Bk., *12); and subsequently noted in the minutes of the Annual General Meeting, 29 June 1885 (*Min. Bk., *26). It was not the only time Strange ran afoul of the Association.*

29. *A copy of Wilson's letter, dated 28 April 1885, is included in the minutes of Annual General Meeting of 29 June 1885 (*Min. Bk., *27).*

1 October 1885

The decision in the *Redemption* case in America [see Feb. 1883] which, it was thought, would protect English copyrighted works, has been unsettled by a totally adverse decision, 17 September, in the 'Mikado case', D'Oyly Carte vs. Duff, tried in a U.S. Circuit Court.[30]

American law seems to be 'delightfully mixed'. Judges of one state of the Union do not recognize decisions in other states; following this latest decision, works with unauthorized orchestrations

30. *Complete text of the judgement is reprinted, p. 23. This and other cases involving Sullivan's compositions are described in detail in Andrew Goodman's* Gilbert and Sullivan at Law *(Rutherford, N.J.: Fairleigh Dickinson Univ. Press [1983]). The* Mikado *case is explained, pp. 208–14 where Sullivan comments on American justice: 'It seemed to be their opinion that a free and independent American citizen ought not to be robbed of his rights of robbing someone else'. (p. 208).*

constructed from the vocal score can be performed in Connecticut and Vermont but are forbidden in Massachusetts. American law gives no protection whatever to the published works of an alien. Sir Arthur Sullivan has gone farther, claiming that neither the U.S. nor Britain gives the protection to copyright 'that is freely offered to the inventor of a new beer-tap'.

The *Mikado* case will probably be carried to the Supreme Court.

L&PMTR, pp. 13, 15, 18, 23

February 1886

Figures on the annual music production in Germany are repeated from the *American Music Journal*. In 1885, 5,474 pieces were issued, the year before, 5,433. Of the 1885 publications, 231 are for symphony orchestra, 51 for band, 406 for single stringed instruments, 111 for single winds, 2,395 for piano, 85 for organs, 1,862 for voice, and the rest miscellaneous. *MO&MTR*, p. 249

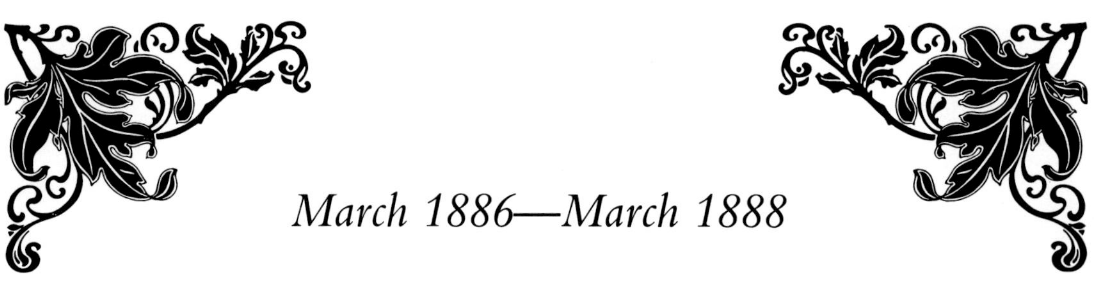

March 1886—March 1888

America 'persists in discreditable isolation'.

Harry Wall 'reserves all his rights', but Stationers' Hall will not disclose what they are.

The 'retrospective' Clause 6 of the Berne Convention alarms the publishers.

The Queen assents to the Berne Convention.

The Music Publishers' Association wants more support.

A 'Lawsuit over a Waltz' reveals publishing costs and pricing practices of music publishers.

The sheet music trade is said to be depressed.

Messrs. Hopwood & Crew is awarded damages but earns a rebuke from the judge.

A ship's steward, Runton, the Song Folio, *the judge in the case and his judgment all attract attention.*

Manuscript copying of copyrighted music elicits warnings from the publishers—again.

1 March 1886

A long article in the *Musical Times* notes the re-emergence of the copyright question about the beginning of February, with a great deal of repetition in articles, letters, and newspapers such as *The Times*, the *Standard*, and the *Daily News*. Most reassuring is the report of the proceedings of the Foreign Office, under Lord Salisbury, which seems to promise a speedy agreement between the chief European States to a copyright convention. Before that can occur, existing British laws in conflict must be removed, and the Incorporated Society of Authors have offered a 'Bill to amend and consolidate laws relating to Copyright'. It does not merely patch up the old and provide 'new machinery: it makes a clean sweep of the whole of them'.[31]

31. *See here the report for 1 August 1886.*

Meantime, in spite of the 'friendly interest' shown by the American delegate to the Berne Conference, America 'will continue to walk alone in the path of self-interest and dishonesty'. American authors and publishers agitate for International Copyright but insist the legislation be one-sided. Matters grow worse and western American publishers now pirate from eastern U.S. music publishers; fees paid by the latter to foreign and native authors 'have touched zero', but it is all done with the blessings of the American Government which 'legalizes plunder'. As Mark Twain pointed out, 'since they were pirates by collusion with the American Government, which made them pirates, they had a right to be pirates'.

Why does America persist in this discreditable isolation and refuse to join her neighbours in the Copyright Convention?

Musical Times, pp. 129–30

25 April 1886

An influential deputation waited upon the President of the Board of Trade on 15 March to urge the codification of the copyright laws and the establishment of an international copyright. The group included artists, authors, publishers, and dramatists, with Mr. Edwin Ashdown and Dr. Villiers Stanford representing musicians. Letters expressing support were presented from Sir Arthur Sullivan, Dr. John Stainer, Edmund Gosse, Willkie Collins, and other eminent persons.

Mr. Underdown, with the guidance of Mr. Mundella's department of the Board of Trade, has prepared a draft bill for discussion. Mr. Underdown assures Mr. Mundella that all of the requirements of the Berne Convention are met by his bill. At the close, the group is assured of Mr. Mundella's support in the present session.

Since the deputation, it has been learned that the bill has been introduced and has passed second reading in the House of Commons. Though a good bill, some points are not touched upon: foreign reprints and their introduction into the Kingdom; the substitution of some Government department for Stationers' Hall where information, for a small fee, can be given the public ('Mr Harry Wall, for example, reserves . . . all his rights, but Stationers' Hall practically refuses to disclose the list of those rights'.); and whether deceased authors should have power to withold their works from the public (public performances of *Parsifal* are prohibited elsewhere than at Bayreuth). *L&PMTR*, pp. 15, 29

June 1886

Clause 6 in the International and Colonial Copyright Bill, which has passed second reading in the House of Commons, has greatly alarmed many by the retrospective rights it creates. Long articles opposing it are reprinted from the *Morning Post* and *Lloyd's Weekly*.[32]

Clause 6 deals with literary, artistic, and musical works; by it pieces of music which have never been copyright in Britain 'will be made copyright'. Foreign works, never copyrighted in England by foreign authors or publishers, but published and copyrighted in England by English firms, would have to be withdrawn or destroyed. Reprints of them would be prohibited. Any which have found their way into anthologies, many for educational purposes, would be protected, making these collections illegal. Works by English composers on which the term of English copyright has expired might still be under long-term copyright in a foreign edition if the retrospective specifications of the bill are applied—to no benefit for the original composer or publisher.[33]

MO&MTR, p. 444

The annual meeting of the MPA, 3 May 1886, first hears the committee's reports about their efforts to gain enforcement of the import duty on American and foreign reprints of English copyrights going into the Cape of Good Hope and Natal. After much correspondence[34] the Treasury reports that the duties collected would be forwarded to the copyright owners.

Still concerned about ships' personnel carrying in illegal reprints, the solicitors have written several Customs Houses and steamship lines for their assistance.

The ubiquitous *Song Folio* remains a problem.[35] An acquaintance of a member is reported to have sent a dozen copies to different addresses in England and Scotland, all of which reached their destination. Questioned about this by the committee, the General Post Office responded that it always stops the *Song Folio*, and that recently several packets of it were disposed of. Pirates in the colony of Victoria have also been active, but the Customs authorities have been helpful and have stopped and destroyed many illegal Ameri-

32. *The 'sweeping changes' of the retrospective clause—'hitherto only heard in Parliament in the small hours of the morning'—are decried also in the* L&PMTR, *15 May 1886 (p. 13). It too reprints the articles from the* Morning Post *and* Lloyd's Weekly.

33. *The problem of retrospective rights is not to be solved until 24 April 1891 in a decision in the Moul vs. Groenings appeal case (see here under 15 May 1891).*

34. *Included in the minutes of the Committee meeting, 5 Oct. 1885* (Min. Bk., *36–38).*

35. *First reported at the MPA meeting of 29 June 1885 in connection with the successful prosecution of Mr. Wilson in Sydney, Australia (see also here the entry for Aug. 1885). The* Song Folio *remained a problem for a long time. Several notices issued by the Association are noted in the* L&PMTR *for 15 Sept. 1890. One begins: 'In regard to the "Song Folio", and other piracies of copyright music—Notice is hereby given . . . .' (See 'Missing Documents', Appendix pp.143–4)*

Forty years later it was still noteworthy. An article about 'Publishers, Printers and Pirates' in the MO&MTR *for October 1925 (pp. 82–83) recalls placidly the days of rampant piracy, the case against Wilson over the 'notorious'* Song Folio, *and closes with congratulations to the MPA for the work it does.*

can reprints, including thousands of copies of *Gems of English Song*—and the *Song Folio*.

After the committee's report, discussion centres on the draft International and Colonial Copyright Bill containing the troublesome clause 6 that offers copyright protection retrospectively. Various members and sub-committees of the Association have met with Lord Arthur Hill and with members of the House of Commons to argue for changes in the clause.[36] Eventually an amendment offered by Mr. Ackland, M.P., was agreed to, though delegates from the Association would have preferred their own. Ackland's alterations do, however, eliminate the major complaints.

36. *The suggested changes appear in the minutes of the Annual General Meeting for 1 June 1886 (*Min. Bk., *59–60).*

The legal proceedings in which the Association has been engaged—with considerable success—have been unduly expensive. The Canadian costs for the case against Strange & Co., alone, reached $440.

It is hinted that the Association may not be certain that it represents a consensus of music publishers' views: 'Your committee regret that the Association does not receive more support from the trade generally, but they [will] continue to exercise that watchfulness and care over the larger interests of the trade . . . feeling sure that the association must eventually receive the cordial and financial support of all music publishers.'[37] *MO&MTR*, pp. 489–90

37. Min. Bk., *60.*

'The Trouble of Copyright' reviews the decision of the jury in the case, Monaghan vs. Taylor.[38] This dealt with infringement of copyright by a singer hired by the proprietor of the Clarence Music Hall in Blackpool, and the jury held the proprietor responsible for the protection of rights in any pieces performed by those he employs. The singer, under the prevailing Copyright Act, is to be considered the agent of the proprietor, and if authorised by the proprietor to sing whatever songs he wishes, the responsibility for the infringement is the proprietor's. *MO&MTR*, pp. 494–95

38. *The case was first heard on 16 January and was earlier reported in the* L&PMTR, *15 Feb. 1886 (pp. 18–19). This retrial took place 31 May and is recounted in the* L&PMTR *of 15 June 1886 (p. 18).*

15 June 1886

Mr. Dixey, Secretary of the Music Publisher's Association, writes to say that the *London & Provincial Music Trades Review* seems unaware of the recent efforts of the Association in regard to the copyright bill and that, in an article in the May issue, 'you are good enough to refer to (it) in terms the reverse of flattering'. A copy of the annual report of the association is enclosed.

The editor responds that since 1884, with the exception of one or two unimportant communications, 'we have heard little or nothing of the Association . . . we could not even find a mention of (it) in this year's musical directories'.

In the following two pages, the magazine prints much of the text of the Association's Annual Report and praises highly the work described there. *L&PMTR*, pp. 18–20

1 August 1886

The Act of Parliament[39] has empowered the Queen to assent to provisions of the Berne Convention on International Copyright within her dominions. The Act repeals all laws inconsistent with its provisions, enacts others limiting and regulating the power of the Queen in Council as regards their applications, and insists on reciprocity.

39. *The International and Colonial Copyright Act of 1886, 49 and 50 Vict., ch. 33.*

Various minor arrangements are included in the twelve sections of the Act, but the great point is that it grants to any author in any country of the Union the same proprietary right in each of the other countries.

'America, true to her selfish policy, holds aloof', but will probably enter the fold when 'it more fully appears that she has something to protect . . .'. *Musical Times*, p. 466

15 April 1887

On 31 March an 'influential deputation from the North of England waited upon Baron H. de Worms' seeking his support for the bill introduced by Mr. Addison, M.P. amending the law of performing rights in musical compositions. The Bill aims to substitute damages as established by a jury for the 40s. penalty and costs which judges are now required to impose.

It used to be that when the right of publication was sold it was understood to cover the performance rights, but of late, those rights have gotten into other hands and innocent people, ignorant of the law, who have sung popular songs at 'penny readings' and the like, have had the 40s. penalty imposed on them, their accompanist, and the giver of the concert.

Mr. Addison's bill would excuse judges from being forced to impose that penalty and would allow them and a jury greater discretion in the matter. For genuine breaches of performing right, 40s. is too mild a fine, but for infringements at penny readings, judge and jury ought to have a range from which to choose.

'The answer to the deputation on behalf of the Government was, of course, marked by official reserve'.[40] *L&PMTR*, p. 13

40. *See here 15 May 1888.*

July 1887

At the annual general meeting of the Music Publishers' Association on 7 June,[41] few matters of grave concern are brought to the floor, but there are several announcements: Strange & Co. of Toronto have infringed another British copyright, have been consulted by a member of the Association, and will cease. The committee has decided to take no special action on a bill relating to the recovery of

41. *Minutes of this meeting (*Min. Bk.*) are the first printed ones (vs. ms.)*

penalties for unauthorized performances of copyrighted works.[42] [No explanation is offered.] The *Song Folio*, *Galaxy of Songs*, and several other piracies coming off the SS. *Galileo* from New York have been detained by Customs at Hull.[43] The committee regrets that the Association has not met with more encouragement but feels sure that it is doing a good job and trust that more extended support will be forthcoming. 'The protection of the best interests of this most important trade has devolved upon but a very small percentage of [the Association's] members'.[44]

MO&MTR, pp. 467–68

42. *A discussion of the bill from the* L&PMTR *is summarized here under 15 April 1887, q.v.*

43. *The subsequent court case is fully reported in the* L&PMTR, *here under 15 Jan. 1888. Note also the entry here under 15 July 1894.*

44. *The complete text of the report is also printed in the* L&PMTR, *15 July 1887 (pp. 19, 21), with editorial comment (pp. 11, 13).*

August 1887

A letter to the Editor and his comments in 'Trade Jottings' point out the decline of profits in sheet music due to competition among the dealers and 'the stores', and the difficulties faced by publishers. Their prices will have to be lowered, though authors' royalties and profits will be made to suffer.[45]

Messrs. Novello & Co. have just published a short history of cheap music as exemplified in the records of their house.[46]

MO&MTR, p. 520

45. *Similar concerns are expressed in correspondence and editorial comments on the problems in the* L&PMTR, *15 July 1887 (p. 11). 'To keep a stock of sheet music in a county wareroom does not now really pay'. The stock is used 'for very little more than a bait to catch piano buyers . . . Dealers have now done almost all they can. Further reply to the question must come from the publishers'.*

46. A Short History of Cheap Music. *(London and New York: Novello, Ewer & Co., 1887). As might be expected in an 1887 publication—except for a note about the famous Gounod* Redemption *case in Boston [see here Feb. 1883]—Novello says little about the copyright and piracy problems covered in this* Chronicle. *Surprisingly, the recent history of the Novello firm by Michal Hurd,* Vincent Novello and Company *(London: Granada [1981]), completely ignores the problems in the* Redemption *case, and more importantly, Novello's key rôle in testing the legality of the American 'manufacture clause' in the U.S. Copyright Act of 1891!*

November 1887

In a 'Lawsuit over a Waltz', the plaintiff, an untutored warehouseman, seeks damages because Doctor Bentley (an examiner in music to the University of Cambridge), whom he had paid to score the piece for pianoforte and for orchestra, had done so 'unskillfully'. [The case is of little importance—except that Bentley seems to have been unfairly treated—but some facts disclosed during its progress are of interest.]

One witness indicates that 'it was a normal thing when waltzes were scored for the pianoforte that they should also be scored for a septet and for the full orchestra'. Messrs. Pitman & Co. agreed to do so, pricing the septet score at £3 10s., the orchestral score at £1 10s. extra. Plaintiff prevailed on Bentley to execute these; there was no formal agreement on price. Plaintiff had 3,000 copies of the pianoforte score (on which Bentley also worked) printed by Heywood & Co., as well as copies of the full score and separate band parts. Plaintiff paid Bentley £5 for it and paid £15 10s. for printing the septet and full orchestral parts, and £20 10s. for the extra parts. 'The septet score was taken from the full score written by the defendant'.

A witness from the printers said only 250 copies of the piano score had been sold and that it was not customary for the composer of a waltz to make any profit out of the band parts. They were sent out gratis to make the waltz popular, to make the piano score and additional band parts sell in profitable quantities.

Witnesses for the two sides testified that Bentley's scoring was either very good or very bad, but the jury, after two or three minutes of deliberation, awarded the warehouseman £50 damages!

MO&MTR, pp. 81–82

In 'Trade Jottings': 'What is to be done with the sheet music trade? Never do we recollect it in such a depressed condition . . . The pianoforte trade, on the contrary, is very busy'.

MO&MTR, p. 87

15 November 1887

Last month's Order in Council will regulate the system of international copyright created at Berne which more than a dozen countries have joined. Austria and the U.S. have not, and citizens of either are, therefore, at liberty to pirate British works.

From the American copyright law [whose chief provisions are quoted], it will be seen that: 1) unless a composer is an American or resides there he cannot have American copyright; 2) American law grants copyrights to foreigners if their works are not printed for publication ('It is for this reason that French plays and full scores are not published at all'); 3) English law gives full copyright to foreigners if their works are first published or performed in this country, but absurdly, works of British composers first performed or published abroad cannot gain British copyright.

L&PMTR, pp. 13, 15

December 1887

Hopwood & Crew are awarded damages in a case involving infringement of twenty-one of their copyrights in the *Popular Sixpenny Song Book* published by George Ingram.[47]

During his examination, Mr. Coote,[48] of Hopwood & Crew, states that he pays from £10 to £100 for the songs he publishes. It costs about 3d to produce each copy, and the net profit is about 1s. per copy. He sometimes makes a profit of £1000 on one song, but the life of these songs is short, from three to four years.

MO&MTR, p. 131

15 December 1887

The Berne Convention between Britain and other countries has gone into effect. The necessary Order in Council (noted in the previous issue) was gazetted on 2 December and the Order came into force on 5 December. Present signatories are Britain, Belgium, France, Germany, Haiti, Italy, Spain, Switzerland, and Tunis.

The article summarizes the provisions of the Convention dealing with literary and artistic works, as well as musical compositions.

L&PMTR, p. 15

47. *A special meeting of the MPA's Committee had been called earlier, 2 Nov. 1886, to discuss this infringement and to order the MPA solicitor to proceed against the vendors (*Min. Bk., *66).*

48. *An interesting aspect of the case is described in the 'Law Report' in the* L&PMTR, *15 Nov. 1887 (p. 15). Mr. Coote had stated that all of his songs bore the legend, 'entered at Stationers' Hall', whether they had been entered or not. The judge cautions that tradesmen run risks 'by telling lies'.*

From the Min. Bk., *85: 'It seems that Messrs. Hopwood & Crew are in the habit of marking all music sold by them with the words, "Entered at Stationers' Hall", whether in fact such had been entered or not and such is believed to be almost a universal custom'.*

Another note about the case from the Min. Bk., *102: '. . . considering the large sum the case against Ingram has cost the Association, the Committee hope [Coote] will follow him up and as they understand he is at his old game again, "that Coote will take him before a magistrate".'*

January 1888
'Trade Jottings' reports that the MPA Committee, at its 20 Dec. 1887 meeting, discussed the growing custom of people making MS. copies of music and ways to inform the public of its illegality.[49] The Committee also resolved that it is inexpedient to give information or legal advice to gentlemen of the trade unless they are members of the Association.[50] *MO&MTR*, p. 182

49. Min. Bk., *88–89. Discussed again in the Committee meeting on 18 Jan. 1888 (*Min. Bk.*, 91–92).*

50. ibid., *87 and 97.*

15 January 1888
A full 'Law Report' and editorial comments are offered about the case Enoch vs. Runton, a steamship steward, who brought into Hull allegedly illegal American reprints of *Song Folio* and other British copyrights. At the trial, Runton declares that he had not brought them in for sale but as presents for his sister. The judge holds this to be a good defence, and a Divisional Court upholds his decision.

The judgement is dangerous, says the editor, for if such a plea gains common acceptance, copyright could be defeated.
L&PMTR, p. 13

In a brief paragraph in 'Our Trade Review', the editor notes some confusion in the minds of more than one member of the Music Publishers' Association about the law concerning MS. copies of copyrighted music. Though it is undoubtedly illegal to copy for purposes of sale, he says, 'there is no law which prevents anybody from copying in MS. any music for his own private use. Any opinion to the contrary is manifestly absurd . . . Music is so cheap that it does not pay to copy it', and as engraved music is so much easier to read than MS., 'both young men and maidens' should prefer it. *L&PMTR*, p. 27

February 1888
'We are informed that Mr. H. Pontet Piccolomini's *Darkness and Light* has reached its fiftieth thousand'. *MO&MTR*, p. 230

15 February 1888
A letter from Mr. George Dixey, Secretary of the Music Publishers' Association, corrects an earlier report by noting that four (not one) copies of an illegal reprint of *The Galaxy of Song* were found by Customs in the steward's quarters, and that they had been 'carefully put away to avoid detection'.[51] At the trial, Enoch vs. Runton, [see 15 Jan. 1888], Runton said they were for his four sisters, but Dixey doubts that.
L&PMTR, p. 21

51. *Letter is in the* Min. Bk., *92–93.*

Elsewhere the editor once more calls the decision in that case a poor one and is pleased to note that the Association proposes to take the case to the Court of Appeal.[52] Were it an illegal amount of tobacco the steward had tried to import without paying duty, the courts would not have asked if it was 'to assist the gentleman's baby boy to cut his teeth', but would have insisted on heavy penalties.

L&PMTR, p. 13

52. *Apparently this was not done. Instead, the Commissioner of Customs was asked to take proceedings against the steward but declined to do so (*ibid., *19).*

March 1888

Edward Ashdown writes: '... I have purchased the entire rights ...' to the piano works of Stephen Heller and the organ pieces of Edouard Batiste, hitherto non-copyright in England. The rights in such works were restored to the composers by the Act of 1886 which went into effect on 6 Dec. 1887 by the Order in Council.[53] Any engraving of the works or arrangements of same after that date infringe Ashdown's copyrights.

A notice from the Music Publishers' Association reminds the public that by virtue of 5 & 6 Vict., cap. 45, sec. 2, making manuscript copies of protected works is illegal and that transcription of copyright songs into other keys is unlawful copying, subject to heavy penalties.[54] *MO&MTR*, p. 277

53. *This is the first notice in the* MO&MTR *of the passage of the important International and Colonial Copyright Act of 1886.*

54. *The same note appears in the* L&PMTR, *15 July 1888 (p. 19) and 15 Sept. 1890 (p. 26). It was earlier discussed in the same magazine for 15 July 1888 (p. 13). 20,000 copies of the notice were sent in parcels to music sellers throughout the Kingdom, but no copies of the notice have been found (See 'Missing Documents', Appendix pp. 143–4).*

15 March 1888

A curious case decided in the Circuit Court in Boston on 29 January presages a similar case in a British court by some eleven years.[55] William Kennedy, and others, owners of the copyright song *Cradle's Empty, Baby's Gone* sue Mr. McTammany, Jr. for reproducing the song on 'perforated sheets'. The judge sees these as part of the machine—'difficult to regard as sheet music'—finds no infringement of copyright, and dismisses the appeal.[56]

The editor fears that English judges will accept the Americans as authorities in the matter. *L&PMTR*, p. 15

55. *See here May 1899.*

56. *The testimony at the trial is summarized in* L&PMTR, *pp. 19, 21.*

May 1888—June 1891

The new Copyright (Musical Composition) Act, 1888, improves performing rights spelling more trouble for Wall and his kind.

The Société des Auteurs, Compositeurs et Éditeurs de Musique gathers strength.

Enoch & Sons' Dance Album *sells 20,000 copies in seven weeks.*

The French want to enforce Clause 6 of the Berne Convention raising Mr. Boosey's ire.

A Music Trade Section of the London Chamber of Commerce is established.

Life's a Game of See-Saw, *a curious case, includes* Ups and Downs *and a fallible memory.*

Adoption of a system of petits droits *in Britain is discussed, and the idea raises Mr. Boosey's ire.*

Lord Monkswell introduces a new copyright bill, the first of many.

A judge thinks an adaptation of a Gilbert adaptation may improve it.

The dangers inherent in Clause 6 of the Berne Convention are effaced by the judgement in the momentous case of Moul vs. Groenings.

15 May 1888

A performing rights bill noted in an earlier issue of *L&PMTR* (15 April 1887) has passed both Houses with few comments and awaits the Royal Assent.[57] It is called the Copyright (Musical Composition) Act, 1888, and it is aimed at those who, having purchased performing rights from composers or others at a small sum, prey on solitary performances at penny readings and charitable entertainments and bring suit against them for penalties and costs. The previous laws did not provide for a jury and left judges no choice but to assess damages for each infringement, however minor or innocent, at 40s, and full costs. For major infringements the fine remained the same! Now a jury and the judge will enjoy alternatives.

Previous to its passage, during the hearings before the Royal Commission on Copyright, Sir Arthur Sullivan, Messrs. Boosey, and others thought that the damages for singing an ordinary song should not amount to more than sixpence; others suggested more seriously that the charge for performances should be legally fixed at that amount. If the fees were enforced by a society such as that in France, considerable sums would be raised for composers. Because of the English royalty system, however, it would be difficult to introduce into England, 'but that is a fair system nobody can deny.'

L&PMTR, pp. 15, 17

57. *The full text is given in the* L&PMTR, *p. 19. It is curious that, during the Music Publishers' Association annual meeting in June 1888, its Committee says it has asked Mr. Addison if he plans to reintroduce the bill in the next session! This is reported in the* L&PMTR, *15 July 1888, p. 21, and in the printed minutes of the Annual General Meeting of the MPA* (Min. Bk., *98*).

The lead article calls attention to a cable from the U.S. declaring that the American Senate on 9 May passed the new copyright bill. It will offer American and English composers reciprocal copyright, but—it appears—no work will be copyright unless it is printed in America from American type.

A warning is offered music publishers not to trust entirely to telegraphic reports but to wait until the full text appears before acting on the new rights.[58]

L&PMTR, p. 11

58. *The warning was prophetic, for indeed such a bill was not signed by a U.S. President until 14 March 1891.*

15 June 1888

At Messrs. Collard's on 28 May, about thirty music publishers meet Mr. Alfred Moul, representative of the Société des Auteurs, Compositeurs et Éditeurs de Musique, and discuss problems which may arise from the Berne Convention.[59]

Mr. Edwin Ashdown in the chair welcomes Mr. Moul warmly, who addresses the group on the Convention and expresses the desire of the foreign musical trade to enter into reciprocal relations with the English trade.

The publishers subsequently pass two resolutions, the first expressing the same hope, the second welcoming and endorsing Mr. Moul's appointment and pledging to assist and encourage his work on reciprocal defence and development.[60]

L&PMTR, pp. 15, 17

59. *The Société, then recently formed, was first mentioned in this chronicle under Aug. 1881, q.v.*

60. *There are no minutes for this meeting in the* Min. Bk. *According to the first item in that book, a clipping, Moul attended the first meeting of the MPA in 1881 and was appointed Secretary of an Association Committee! The friendliness with Moul from that time to this did not last through 1888; see Dec. 1888 entry.*

September 1888

Enoch & Sons' *The Dance Album* has reached its twentieth thousand in seven weeks. *MO&MTR*, p. 562

15 November 1888

In a brief paragraph about a composer who publishes successfully his own compositions, it is noted that Sir Arthur Sullivan usually proceeds on the royalty system. For some of his songs on which vocalists' royalties are no longer paid, he receives 7d. for each copy sold. Most publishers follow a mixed system: the words are bought outright and the composer receives a small sum down with a 2d. or 3d. royalty. The numbers are 'checked by the composer himself who stamps his name or initials on every title-page'.

L&PMTR, p. 25

December 1888

Mr. Boosey writes to the *Era* to remind managers of theatres and music halls that the works of foreign composers, under the Berne Convention of 1886, may command a fee for performance in English places of entertainment. The rule applies to operas, vocal selections therefrom, and minor compositions such as waltzes, songs, and polkas that managers used to have unrestricted freedom to perform. It is no longer necessary to enter compositions at Stationers' Hall; consequently, it will be difficult for managers to ascertain what is freely available.[61]

Mr. Boosey has unkind words for 'our neighbours (who mean to insist on their extreme rights) . . . vexatious rights of performance that have never been, and never will be, understood here. They must not be pained or surprised if their work is excluded in favor of that of native composers'. *MO&MTR*, pp. 139–40

15 December 1888

During a copyright case, G. W. Hunt vs. Fineburg et al., on 6 December, the judge refers to the infamous Harry Wall. The solicitor for the defendants in this case asks the judge to dismiss the action because it had been commenced by Wall in the name of Grayston, a solicitor who had allowed Wall to use his name improperly. The judge does so, pointing out that in August Grayston had been suspended from practice for two years and that Wall, for acting as a solicitor when not duly qualified, had been sentenced to three months' imprisonment.[62] *L&PMTR*, p. 20

28 December 1888

[Not reported in any of the journals—appearing only in the minutes of the MPA's Annual General Meeting for 13 June 1889—was a meeting of London music publishers held at the MPA offices on 28

61. *It is, in fact, a correspondence between Boosey and Mr. Moul, representative of the Société des Auteurs, Compositeurs et Éditeurs de Musique, who was so warmly received by the music publishers at a meeting a few months earlier (see entry for 15 June 1888). The exchange is also extensively reported and quoted from in the* L&PMTR, *15 Dec. 1888, pp. 13, 15.*

62. *A later copyright case heard on 12 February, Irving vs. Sanger, is also thrown into turmoil by Grayston and Wall's earlier activities. It is reported in* L&PMTR, *15 Feb. 1888 (p. 21). In the same place (p.22) appears a long account of the appeal in Hunt vs. Fineburg.*

The infamous, though not well-known Wall, flits in and out of discussions of copyright, and long before this date, 1888, he was notorious. The MO&MTR *article on 'Musical Copyright' in April 1878, for example, notes the 'Harry Wall proceedings'. See more here in note 7 at Nov. 1881 and the report at 15 April 1887.*

December 1888 'to consider the prevalent practices of underselling by the trade ... After considerable discussion the matter was dropped'.

On the few occasions when this topic came up it was pushed aside. Despite the agitation and outcries from musicsellers, many of them appearing as letters to editors of trade journals, it was obviously a problem the MPA never intended to confront, much less solve.]

March 1889

The advisability of establishing a Music Trade Section of the London Chamber of Commerce was considered at a meeting on 29 January, E. Ashdown in the chair.[63] Eighteen music publishers and instrument makers attended the session. In his opening remarks Mr. Ashdown cannot resist complaining anew about the Order in Council issued thirty years ago allowing the colonies to import piratical copies: 'The present position of musical copyright in the colonies [is] most unsatisfactory'.

Returning to the purpose of the meeting, those present resolve to join the Chamber of Commerce and to establish a Provisional Committee formed of eight publishers and seven instrument makers to organize the section, pursue its business, and to persuade other firms to join.

The *MO&MTR* prints a later report of this Provisional Committee in which it indicates that those actions have been taken and that the number of members has grown to thirty-six. Another meeting for 26 February is announced. *MO&MTR*, pp. 292–93

63. *Minutes for this 29 January meeting are not preserved in the* Min. Bk., *but those for an earlier meeting, 28 Dec. 1888, remark the attendance of the Secretary of the Chamber of Commerce and his plea for support (*Min. Bk., *106).*

A few pages later, the *MO&MTR* summarizes that 26 February meeting, quoting at length some of the discussion. Most of the remarks emanate from the instrument manufacturers who state—acrimoniously—that they see no fair representation for themselves with only one representative, a publisher, from the Music Trade Section sitting on the Chamber's Council. The concerns of the two groups are widely divergent, they claim, implying that they are irreconcilable;[64] the publishers are interested in copyright problems, the manufacturers with the 'three-year' system and hire agreements. Mr. Wallis, a manufacturer, is especially upset and blunt: 'Some of us have joined under false pretences'. Mr. Chappell woefully declares, 'We shall not be able to do anything for either trade this year', but a working committee is elected, nevertheless, and a future meeting is discussed.[65] *MO&MTR*, p. 308

64. *A more sanguine view of these differences is found in a leading article in the* L&PMTR, *15 Mar. 1889 (p. 13, 15), a more objective summary of the 26 Feb. meeting,* ibid. *(pp.18, 19).*

65. *Minutes of the meeting are not in the* Min. Bk.

The provisions of the Berne Convention remain troubling to the British music trade, British performers and entrepreneurs. Some foreign copyright holders intend to collect fees for the performance of their properties which have been restored to copyright by the Act. The retrospective force couched in clause 6[66]—about which so much argument and manoeuvring has already taken place—remains, even as amended, the troublesome part of the law.[67]

Performing rights are ambiguously set out in the law, and one expert has stated that he doubts whether such general expressions as 'tous droits réserves', or 'propriété pour tous pays', satisfy the requirements of this clause. These matters will probably be settled in the courts.[68] *MO&MTR*, p. 296

The French and British systems are contrasted. In France the composer receives a small fee for each performance, collected for him by a society.[69] In England, publishers pay vocalists to popularize a song, either by a specified fee per night or a royalty on copies sold, for a specified term or perhaps for the duration of the copyright. Vocalists stamp their name on each copy in order to check the numbers sold, the much-criticized 'royalty system'.

MO&MTR, p. 296

15 March 1889

On 13 February, Mr. Moul, representative of the Société des Auteurs, Compositeurs et Éditeurs de Musique, brings action for infringement of copyright in Westminster County Court.[70] One case, Moul vs. Hawtrey and Corri (Hawtrey, the lessee of, and Corri, the conductor at, the Strand); the other, uncontested is Moul vs. Squire and Lennard. These are the first attempts to enforce the retrospective protection contained in the Berne Convention. Fortunately, the County Court is not a Court of Record and, therefore, the decisions for plaintiffs cannot be cited as authority by any other court. Unfortunately, the solicitors for defence in Moul vs. Hawtrey cite the wrong law to support their contention that the music from which the defendants took a melody (less than 22 bars) should have had printed upon it a warning that performing rights were reserved. Plaintiff argues that this provision is contained in the Copyright Act of 1882, but that statute was not incorporated into the Convention, therefore it did not apply. What the judge and others seem not to know is that the Convention's own Article 9 demands the same warning. Unless a copyright owner expressly forbids public performance, he has no right to sue for infringement. Nevertheless, the judge's decision is for Moul. *L&PMTR*, pp. 15, 21

Judgement is given in the *Life's a Game of See-Saw* case. The defendant says that this song, whose copyright he is accused of

66. *49 & 50 Vict., ch. 33, sec. 6 is explained here under June 1886 and is discussed in the* L&PMTR, *15 July 1888 (p. 11).*

67. *See also here under 15 May 1891.*

68. *Most of these same points are the subject of leading articles in the* L&PMTR, *15 Feb. 1889 (pp. 11, 13).*

69. *The Société des Auteurs, Compositeurs et Editeurs de Musique. A valuable history of the organization and comprehensive description of the system of* petits droits *is offered in the report of a court case, the Société vs. Chappell & Co. in the* L&PMTR, *15 April 1900 (pp. 23, 25) and 15 June 1900 (p. 30).*

70. *Also reported in an article in* Musical Times, *March 1889 (pp. 137–38).*

infringing, is really an old one played at Norwich in 1855–56 under the title *Ups and Downs*. Later, called *Life's a Scene of Ups and Downs* by William West, it was published by Williams in 1871; then as *Life's a Game of Ups and Downs* by Arthur Lloyd, published by D'Alcorn in 1873; and finally, as *Life's Like a Game of See-Saw* by G. W. Hunt, published by Hopwood & Crew in 1877.

The judge states in his decision for the plaintiff that the evidence to support this is very unsatisfactory, and that he cannot rely on the defendant's memory. *L&PMTR*, pp. 21–22

15 April 1889

The first meeting of the Committee of the Music Trades Section of the London Chamber of Commerce is held on 26 March with Edwin Ashdown presiding.[71] Among the subjects identified for discussion are: 1) the copyright questions; 2) railway rates; 3) registration of bills of sale; 4) performing rights; 5) the British and Irish Industry Bill; 6) the Merchandise Marks Act; and 7) American consular fees and regulations.

At another meeting on 9 April it is decided to split the Committee into two sub-sections representing the music publishers and the musical instrument manufacturers which will each meet separately in the future. *L&PMTR*, p. 31

71. *In an editorial on the swift progress of the Committee in its 15 May 1889 issue (p. 11), the editor calls Ashdown a 'gentleman of large views and liberal mind', and notes that he is also President of the Music Publishers' Association.*

15 May 1889

'The New York *Musical Courier* reports the incorporation at Springfield, Illinois, on the 5th ult. of a limited liability company entitled "United States Vogel Kazophone and Electrical Microphone Trumpet Aucastic Electromotor Power Musical Car Distance Loud Speaking Transfer Instrument Company of Chicago"; capital, $65,000,000.' *L&PMTR*, p. 26

15 July 1889

A paragraph in 'Our Trade Review' suggests that British publishers, whose music has been so heavily pirated in America, may be pleased 'to find their American brethren similar sufferers'.

According to the *Chicago Indicator*, Oliver Ditson Co. of Boston has filed suit in the District Court in Detroit against a music dealer there seeking seizure and forfeiture of a stock of pirated editions of works by L. M. Gottschalk and G. D. Wilson brought in from Germany. In the 'descent on the music store' by the U.S. Marshal, about 100 pieces were seized. Since U.S. law requires a fine of 4s. for each sheet of contraband printings, and these pieces consist of from five to ten sheets each, it is apt to be expensive for the dealer.

L&PMTR, p. 31

15 September 1889

A *Musical Times* editorial calls attention to a practice, 'which is growing every day more pronounced, of reproducing in manuscript copyright works'. Three types of offenders are singled out: 1) the young lady[72] who, just having purchased a copyright song, makes a copy for her accompanist or circulates it to her friends; 2) the parson who buys a Service or an Anthem and re-copies it until he has supplied each member of the choir; 3) the enthusiastic organizer of local concerts. The usual excuses—ignorance of the law, not knowing a work is copyrighted, or feelings that 'the law is absurd'—are examined and dismissed as nonsensical.

72. *cf. here Dec. 1882, Mar. 1883, and Mar. 1888.*

Musical Times, pp. 535–36

A new copyright bill has passed the Canadian Parliament and awaits the royal assent. Considerable outcry has been raised about it by British music publishers. 'The history of copyright in Canada would not be particularly interesting reading'; in practice, Canadian dealers freely deal in American piratical reprints of British copyrights, and the royalties on those imposed by their laws are rarely forthcoming. Whatever the new law says, the situation can hardly worsen.[73]

73. *In its Annual Report for 1889 and 1890 in the* Min. Bk.*—in the latter in bold face type—the MPA calls it 'simple confiscation of English rights'. Included in the* Min. Bk. *is Clayton's article on Anglo-Canadian copyright, clipped from the* Musical Times.

Its principal provisions grant Canadian copyright to citizens in Berne Convention countries on condition that they register the work in Canada before or simultaneously with publication abroad, or that they reprint or publish it in Canada within one month of publication elsewhere. If this is not done, the Minister of Agriculture [!] may grant a licence to a Canadian to reprint or publish the work who will pay the author ten per cent on the retail price through the Inland Revenue.

Other clauses give the Government power to prohibit (or allow) importation of unauthorized copies if licensees do (or do not) meet adequately the public demand. The Government may also prohibit any importation of British copyrights.

Ten per cent royalty, the writer thinks, is a generous figure that should please both British composer and copyright owner.

L&PMTR, p. 13

15 October 1889

W. S. Gilbert has sought an interlocutory injunction to restrain Messrs. Boosey & Co. from using his name in connection with an altered libretto of *Les Brigands*. Gilbert adapted this work for Boosey some twenty years ago from Offenbach's opera to a libretto by Meilhac and Halévy. Boosey was assigned all rights to the adaptation by Gilbert at that time.

A current production in London omits one solo and has added

two songs. To Gilbert's solicitor's claims that such alterations could not be done if his name was still to be used in the production, the printed libretto, and in advertisements, the judge responds that Gilbert has no control over it, having previously assigned all the rights. Furthermore, it is suggested that the changes made by those producing such a work may, in fact, improve it, to Mr. Gilbert's ultimate benefit. So long as the changes are not made in bad faith and do not injure the reputation of the author, no trifling changes justify the injunction awarded and it is dissolved.[74]

L&PMTR, pp. 15, 21, 23

74. *On appeal, 6 November, this decision was upheld. Reported* ibid., *15 November 1889 (p. 25).*

15 December 1889

A brief paragraph notes that U.S. Postal authorities have given general orders to stop all foreign music entering the U.S. and for American copyright music republished abroad to be sent back. Such a general order dealing with American piratical reprints has been in force for a long time in England.

Another short paragraph reports that on 12 December several composers and publishers held a meeting to found a society for the collection of fees as is done in France by the Société des Auteurs, Compositeurs et Éditeurs de Musique. A committee is appointed to prepare a report for submission at another, later meeting.[75]

L&PMTR, p. 29

75. *See following report.*

15 January 1890

Last month a private meeting was held by a large number of composers, librettists and music publishers to discuss the inauguration of a system of *petits droits* in England. Some large firms were represented, among others, Chappell, Ashdown, Novello, Hopwood & Crew, R. Cocks, and Patey & Willis. Few composers but a large number of librettists attended. Besides a resolution favouring the establishment of the French system of fixed fees for performance of ballads and separate songs, a committee of nine was chosen to draw up a report for a subsequent meeting in January.

Since then two of the largest song publishers, Boosey and J. B. Cramer, have protested the decisions and have indicated publicy they will not participate, which may make the plan difficult to carry out. The next meeting upon a subject in which the public are so deeply interested should be an open one, 'the reports duly published', says the editor. *L&PMTR*, pp. 15, 17

15 February 1890

Lord Monkswell has introduced into the House of Lords a Bill that will not only amend the law of copyright but will consolidate all previous acts and contain the whole law on the subject. Its provisions are described in some detail; in summary, they include: 1) copyright exists for the life of the composer and thirty years; on anonymous works, for thirty years after publication; 2) registration is made compulsory but ('a blot on the bill') foreign copyrights need not be; 3) a Government Register is to substitute for the Stationers' Hall as the place of registration; 4) copies required by universities and libraries as part of registration must still be delivered; 5) 'copyright' is defined; 6) 'Performing right' is defined; 7) arrangements and adaptations may be copyrighted by any person with the consent of the owner of the original copyright; 8) works by British subjects first published or performed abroad may obtain copyright by republishing within three years in the U.K.; 9) assignment of copyright of a book containing a musical work or of a separate composition does not convey performing rights; 10) piratical reprints are infringements of copyright; 11) for infringement, authors may enter an action or apply for an injunction, and every piratical copy is to be forfeited to the copyright owner; 12) copyright may be registered within one month of the first publication.

The Bill is intricate and the writer of the article expects objections on many points to 'occur to music publishers'.

L&PMTR, pp. 13, 15

A conference between representatives of the Music Publishers' Association and the Provincial Music Trades Association will be held later this month to discuss publishers 'giving the dealers increased facilities for ordering and reordering sheet music, operas, etc.' In response to a circular from the Secretary of the MPA,[76] most dealers have written to say they have stopped selling sheet music. It is a branch of the trade 'which implies a maximum of trouble with a minimum of profit'. Sheet music is distributed to the largest purchasers (schools and others) direct from the publishers and the Co-operative stores do the rest. Provincial dealers' stocks are used mainly by purchasers to select what to buy from the stores. *L&PMTR*, pp. 13, 15

76. *No copy of the original found. See 'Missing Documents', Appendix pp. 143–4).*

15 April 1890

Mr. E. Ashdown, presiding over the annual meeting of the Music Trade Section of the London Chamber of Commerce on 28 March, reports that the Canadian government's proposals dealing with copyright are under consideration and that a deputation has waited on Lord Knutsford on the subject. From that meeting he thinks the Canadian people will be allowed to do just what they please; 'the British government could not afford to offend the Canadians'.

A sub-committee of the music publishers has drafted a bill intended to protect the public 'from vexatious proceedings for the recovery of performing fees', i.e., *petits droits*. Mr. Boosey urges that its introduction and passage be pursued, but the Chairman thinks it best to 'let it remain for the present'.

The French music publishers are about 'to wake up the Berne Convention business', and the sub-committee has sent a letter to Lord Salisbury warning him that the French may try to alter Article XIV of the Convention which grants reciprocal rights, subject to specified conditions, to authors in signatory countries. Lord Salisbury replies that no communication has been received from the French government on the subject, but the matter will be 'borne in mind'.[77] *L&PMTR*, pp. 19, 21

77. *Subsequent letters to and from the Sub-committee and Lord Salisbury are reprinted in the* L&PMTR *for 15 May 1891 (p. 23).*

15 May 1890

A letter from Boosey & Co. complains about 'the inconvenience and annoyance already caused to the public by the demand of the Société des Auteurs, Compositeurs et Éditeurs de Musique for fees upon works which have been freely performed here for years, their demand, of course, being based upon the recent signing of the Berne Convention by us'.

The firm has addressed the problems in a letter to the French publisher, Heugel [which is reprinted]. Its final paragraph predicts that, unless French composers and publishers reconsider, an association of English concert-managers and concert-givers will exclude from their programmes all those smaller foreign works upon which the *petits droits* are demanded. *L&PMTR*, p. 31

15 June 1890

Letters and editorials comprising an acrimonious exchange between Sydney Ashdown and the Toronto *Evening Telegram* are printed. The issues are the provisions of the new Canadian copyright bill, which the *Telegram* first criticized under the caption, 'Want the Whole Earth?' After several letters from Ashdown and editorial rejoinders from the *Telegram*, the paper states, 'The Canadian Copyright act will pass in time . . . The Canadian Government have the power to pass their own laws, including those on copyright . . . The English book trade apparently think that Canada "as a colony" should be entirely at their mercy . . . We propose to have the same rights as Americans . . .'

Though it is true that Canada has been overrun for a long time with American piracies, cheap reprints of English copyrights, the debate scarcely contributes to a solution. *L&PMTR*, pp. 15, 17

15 September 1890

[The following notices have been issued by the Music Publishers' Association in regard to the *Song Folio* and other piracies, and to music copying. The notice regarding music copying was approved at the MPA Committee meeting on 18 Jan. 1888 (*Min. Bk.*, 91–92). The decision to print it on 'the same card' is recorded in the minutes for the meeting of 8 July 1890 (*Min. Bk.*, 122). No copies of the original found (see 'Missing Documents', Appendix).]

The following notices have been issued by the Music Publishers' Association. In regard to 'The Song Folio,' and other piracies of copyright music—"Notice is hereby given, that by virtue of 5 & 6 Vict., cap. 45, sec. 23, any person having in his possession 'The Song Folio,' or any other book containing copyright music unlawfully printed or imported without the written consent of the proprietor of the copyright therein, is liable to action at law to compel the delivery up of such book and the payment of damages to the proprietor of the copyright."

MUSIC COPYING.

Notice is hereby given that by virtue of the 5 & 6 Vict., cap. 45, sec. 2, the sole and exclusive liberty of making manuscript or other copies of copyright works is vested in the owner of such copyright, and any other persons making such copies without the permission of the said owner render themselves liable to heavy penalities or damages.

The transposition of copyright songs into other keys is an unlawful copying. By order,

G. DIXEY,

Secretary Music Publishers' Association.

9, Air Street, Regent Street, W., Jan. 1888.

October 1890

J. A. Cross of Manchester writes about a 'new terror', an outgrowth of the provisions of the Berne Convention. Cross has lost a case in Manchester dealing with infringement of performing rights. The 'new terror' he points to is a French society for the protection of foreign performing rights which claims to have a list of thousands of pieces so protected, but, he says, 'no list can be procured'. Unless a fee is paid—a fee determined by the society's agent, covering a given period of time—'you are liable to be pounced upon for performing any one of these thousands of pieces . . . The society are not even obliged to print the reservation on the music in this country, some kind of order in council overruling the act in that respect'. Cross, a concert giver, has 'withstood' the society so far and refuses to pay what they call the licence fee.[78]

MO&MTR, p. 31

78. *This case was described in 'Our Law Reports' and analyzed in an editorial in the* L&PMTR *for 15 Sept. 1890 (pp. 17–18). An earlier case brought by the Society—'Moul and Others vs. Devonshire Park and Megone'—was recounted in the* L&PMTR *for 15 Jan. 1890 (pp. 11, 21). Plaintiffs in that trial included Delibes, Thomas, Massenet, Gounod, Saint-Saëns, and the heirs of Bizet. Witnesses for the defence included William Boosey, S. A. Chappell, and Oliver Hawkes.*

March 1891

'Extracts from the London Correspondence of the *American Art Journal*' first notes the alarms expressed by English publishers over the proposed new American copyright bill. A meeting of the music trade and allied sections of the London Chamber of Commerce has vigorously denounced the clauses which compel music sold in America to be printed from types engraved or cut in the U.S.[79]

Also reported are efforts being made to bring the interests of provincial dealers and London publishers closer. The sale of sheet music has not been profitable for the dealers. Marked at 4s. or 3s., it is always sold to the public at half price. Teachers usually purchase copies for one-third the marked price, but lately, co-operative stores have been offering that same price to all customers.

To discuss this problem and others, a conference between some members of the Provincial Trades Association and the Music Publishers' Association was held in the spring. The outcome has encouraged dealers to again stock sheet music; they will be offered more liberal terms.

The writer of the report thinks that 'sooner or later the American system of cheap music must be adopted . . . Any song or pianoforte piece should . . . be sold for sixpence'. *MO&MTR*, pp. 231–32

79. *Reported also in* L&PMTR, *15 Dec. 1890 (p. 15), and again, 15 Jan 1891 (p. 13).*

April 1891

The U.S. Congress passed[80] and President Harrison signed on 14 March the American Copyright Act of 1891. It offers the first legal recognition of British (and other foreign) composers' property rights in the U.S. Those writers can now sell the exclusive rights to their works to American publishers in return for lump sum payments or for royalties, profits heretofore gathered by the pirates. The bill, unfortunately, contains the American 'manufacture clause',[81] because the engravers and publishers would support the measure only in that form. The American *Evening Post* calls the clause 'a piece of tariff barbarism calculated to make one hang the head'.[82] *MO&MTR*, p. 272

80. *'. . . a few minutes before its adjournment' on 4 March, according to* L&PMTR, *15 March 1891 (p. 11). Cf. entry here for September 1906! The article also comments on some aspects of the bill not mentioned by the* MO&MTR.

81. *These clauses are transcribed and discussed in a long article, 'The New American Copyright Act',* ibid., *15 April 1891 (pp. 11, 13).*

82. *For a more optimistic interpretation of the Act's effects on Britons, see C. Nicholl's article in the* Musical News *1 (10 April 1891): 109–10.*

15 May 1891

The Music Publishers Subsection Committee of the London Chamber of Commerce has held five meetings to consider the provisions of Lord Monkswell's Consolidation Bill, introduced over a year ago. As suggested in a report in the *L&PMTR*, 15 Feb. 1890 [q.v.], many objections to the provisions have 'occurred' to the publishers and they are presented, along with some suggested amendments. 'The most important alterations are in regard to the law of foreign and colonial copyright'. The subcommittee agrees unanimously that clauses 55 to 66 should be struck out, 'thereby retaining intact the Copyright Act of 1886[83] and the Orders in

83. *The International Copyright Act of 1886.*

Council passed thereunder.'

The subcommittee wants Section 88 to require not only the forfeiture of unlawful copies, but also the plates from which the copies were produced, and to authorize searches by peace officers of any place 'where it may be reasonably suspected that pirated wares are held for sale'.

In Section 89, the subcommittee wants not only the power to seize unlawful copies 'when hawked about for sale', but a provision permitting illegal copies to be taken before a court of summary jurisdiction and then, upon proof of their illegality, delivered up to the owner of the copyright.

The Bill is necessarily complicated because Lord Monkswell seeks to repeal and consolidate all previous copyright legislation, as well as a bill being offered concurrently by the Society of Authors.

L&PMTR, pp. 3, 5, 7

The 'retrospective force' of clause 6 of the Berne Convention, which has troubled British publishers since it was first introduced, is finally dealt with in the case of Mayeur [i.e., Moul!] vs. Groenings in the Divisional Court, on appeal from the Brighton County Court.[84] The French Society will probably carry it farther, to the Court of Appeal, but for now, a county court judge and two justices of the Queen's Bench Division have held that 'though concert-givers and publishers who, before December 1887, had performed or published ... non-registered French works had had no absolute "rights", yet they had a "legal interest subsisting and valuable", and cannot be held liable retrospectively for fees'.

L&PMTR, pp. 13, 18–19

84. *The outcome of the case is also noted in* Musical News *1 (1 May 1891): 168*

The music publishers, still concerned that the French publishers are attempting to modify the Berne Convention—as well as clause 6 of the Copyright Act of 1886—have written Lord Salisbury again (22 Nov. 1890), repeating the apprehensions voiced a few months ago. Again Lord Salisbury replies (26 Nov. 1890) that H.M. Government has received no representations from the French, but the 'subject will be borne in mind'.[85] A verbatim 'Report of the Music Publishers Sub-Section for the Year 1890–91' includes the letters.

L&PMTR, pp. 15, 23

85. *cf. 15 April 1901.*

15 June 1891

As anticipated in the previous month's columns, the French Society has taken the case of Moul (sic) vs. Groenings, the Brighton Pier Bandmaster, to the Court of Appeal, and again the courts have held for the defendant's rights to freely perform previously non-copyright French music. The editor comments that the decision may be even more important for those who have published non-copyright French music.[86] The Court's judgement seems to extend British rights farther than previous interpretations by implying that when an English publisher has acquired the right to sell copies, he has also the rights of performance. *L&PMTR*, pp. 15, 18

86. *On these points, the decisions in this case are greatly amplified by the judgment in the Lauri vs. Renaud appeal, 3 June 1892. The Justices rule, categorically, that section 6 of the Berne Convention does not 'restore the copyright in any work which has been produced or published before the passing of the Act in 1886'. The decision is reprinted in the* L&PMTR *for 15 June 1892 (p. 13).*

Moul vs. Groenings is also cited later in a judgment handed down by Mr. Justice Chitty in Schauer vs. *Field, 31 Oct. 1892 (and reviewed in the* L&PMTR *for 25 Nov. 1892, p. 11). The German firm applied unsuccessfully for an injunction to restrain the defendant from printing a picture they claimed was restored to copyright by the Convention.*

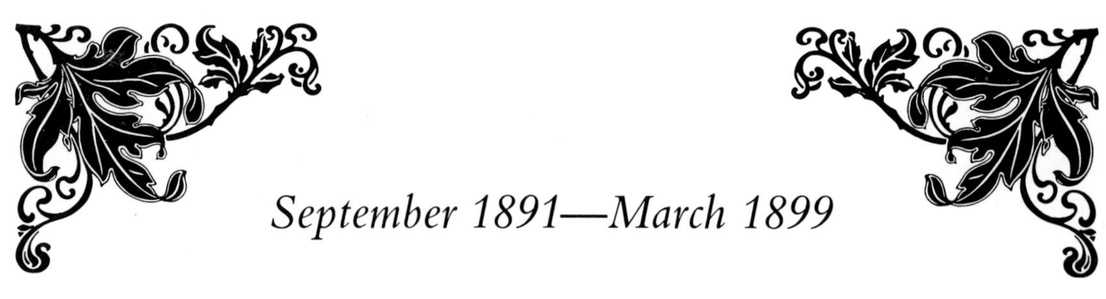

September 1891—March 1899

The new U.S. Copyright Bill is hailed 'with glee'.

The Canadian Parliament seeks copyright independence—from just about everyone.

A 'friendly' transatlantic 'action' seeks to clarify the U.S. law.

A music publisher says he has 210,000 customers' names in thirty-five volumes housed in a strong room.

The MPA continues to issue notices about the ubiquitous Song Folio.

The cost of publishing in France and the workings of petits droits *are thoroughly explained.*

Amendments to the Canadian Copyright Act are passed and await the Royal Assent (aggravation upon aggravation!).

Annoyed musicsellers ask publishers about their practices and receive churlish answers for their trouble.

Three Canadian pirates in Toronto hurt U.S. trade.

Publishers accuse the dealers of underselling to the trade; the dealers retort.

The new American Copyright Bill may reinstitute the 'Manufacture clause'.

Publishers toughen their stance and their actions on piracies.

By one estimate, 20 million pieces of music are sold in England in 1898.

'Rex' estimates that 8,500,000 copies of new music are 'thrown upon' the market by British music publishers each year.

September 1891
'London music publishers ... hail with glee the passage of the International Copyright Bill' in the U.S. Congress. Librarian of Congress Spofford has interpreted the law to exclude music from those publications (for example, books) that must be manufactured in the U.S. to be suitable for U.S. copyright protection.[87] 'They are not required to be of American manufacture'. Music printed in London from British plates can now be copyright in the U.S., diminishing the piratical procedure of American publishers printing British music from American plates without paying royalties to British composers or firms. *MO&MTR*, p. 477

87. *The bill was signed into law by the President on 1 July 1891, according to the* L&PMTR *of 15 July 1891 (p. 28). C. Nicholls in an earlier issue of the* Musical Times, *17 July 1891, had analysed the bill thoroughly. Its passage is hailed by the* Musical Times *in the issue for 17 July 1891. While also acclaiming its passage in its issue of 15 July 1891, the* L&PMTR *wonders (p. 13) whether pieces of music with words will be considered 'books.'*

15 September 1891
In a note to the journal, *L'art musical* [reprinted in translation], Mr. Victor Souchon, Agent-General of the society of Authors, Composers and Editors of Music in Paris, recounts the background to the recent cases of Mayeur (*sic*)[88] vs. Groenings, and emphasizes his organization's dismay at the decisions of the English courts: 'In order not to affect the rights of a publisher who plays the *rôle* of a pirate, the English law recognizes his publication as lawful ... They have confiscated an object at the moment when such confiscation is lawful'.

88. i.e. *Moul.*

The article in *L'art musical* says that Mr. Souchon will make new efforts through the French Ministry, will address the subject before the Congress of Artistic Property,[89] and will carry his complaints to the delegates meeting in 1892 or 1893 in Paris to revise the Berne Convention.

89. i.e., *the Congress of the International Literary and Artistic Association's meeting at Neuchatel, 26 Sept.–3 Oct. 1891. Souchon did deliver a paper about English copyright.*

The English editor's comments include a hope that 'the French will first be compelled to register their copyrights here, so that innocent English performers and publishers may know whether the work is duly protected'. *L&PMTR*, p. 15.

October 1891
Morley & Co. secure the first British entry under the new American copyright act, for J. Vale Lane's *For Thee Valses* on 6 July. *MO&MTR*, p. 37

15 October 1891
In a letter to the *L&PMTR*, Kenric B. Murray, Secretary of the London Chamber of Commerce, discusses the recent surprising proceedings in the Canadian Parliament which subsequently addressed the Queen asking the Imperial Parliament to 'confer upon Canada the power to legislate upon the subject of copyright without regard to the statutes in force when the Parliament in Canada was established'. If carried out, he says, their action will be most prejudicial to British copyright owners. 'While all Europe is

doing its utmost to induce the U.S. to join the Berne Convention, Canada, an English colony, is taking steps to withdraw'.

He also reminds readers that not long ago, the Canadian Copyright Act of 1889 was refused the royal assent,[90] 'but the agitation has again broken out'. *L&PMTR*, pp. 18–19

90. *Announced in bold-face type in the minutes of the MPA Annual General Meeting, 3 June 1890 (*Min. Bk.*, 117).*

January 1892

As reported in a New York paper: The new international copyright law produces curious complications and results. American music publishers flock to Britain; London publishers establish New York City offices;[91] competition between them grows; composers in Britain and the U.S. both lose and profit. Some London writers organize to protect their American rights, and to force payment for American sales, while American composers, whose works are not protected in England, regret that the U.S. is not a signatory to the Berne Convention. *MO&MTR*, p. 152

91. *One of three good methods to take advantage of the new situation suggested in an earlier editorial in the* L&PMTR *for 15 Sept. 1891 (p. 13).*

15 April 1892

A challenge to English publishers in regard to the American Copyright Act has been begun by the Americans. The *American Art Journal* reports that, on behalf of the Oliver Ditson Co., the Boston music printer, F. H. Gilson Co., has sent to Novello's New York branch reprints of four of Novello's English copyrights, including *Lead, Kindly Light.* Novello's New York manager has sent the music to the London headquarters. It will be a month before the case can come up in the courts, perhaps six for settlement.[92]

L&PMTR, pp. 31, 33

92. *In an editorial a few months later in the* L&PMTR *for 15 Aug. 1892 (p. 11), the case is referred to as 'a* bona fide*, but otherwise friendly' action between Novello of London and Ditson of Boston. Its intent, according to a note in the* Musical News *4 (5 Aug. 1892): 126–27, is 'to test the legality of the clause in the new [American] copyright law, which the American houses maintain directs that musical compositions must be engraved and printed in the U.S.' in order to be protected by that law.*

15 June 1892

The annual meeting of the Music Trades Section of the London Chamber of Commerce takes place on 2 June, Mr. William Boosey presiding. A long report from the Music Publishers' Sub-Section is presented by Mr. C. E. Musgrave, its Assistant Secretary. The Sub-Section has met only once in the past year, but its representatives have met with the Joint Copyright Committee of the Chamber. The Sub-Section's only meeting was on 8 June with the Printing and Allied Trades Section to consider promoting a new Copyright Amendment Bill now that Lord Monkswell's Consolidation Bill has been withdrawn. Eight meetings, it is recalled, were held during 1890–91 considering amendments to the Consolidation Bill, for naught. Lord Balfour of Burleigh's late suggestion in the House that a short bill be prepared for introduction was discussed at the 8 June meeting.

Lord Monkswell's Bill was 'essentially an author's measure, and . . . publishers . . . have not lost much by its withdrawal'.

Several questions are to be dealt with in the coming year: American copyright, which is in a very complicated position; the right of aliens to have copyright in Britain without residence (a difficulty about which the American publishers are alive); and the Canadians' efforts to separate themselves from copyright in the mother country. The Performing Rights Bill prepared by Mr. Fitzgerald 'had better stand over', since the decision in the case of Herr Groenings seems to have eliminated the evil which brought it forth.

L&PMTR, pp. 21, 23

15 August 1892

The Music Publishers' Association has broadcast to music publishers a circular outlining their actions in preparation for the Novello vs. Ditson case in America.[93] Mr. L. L. Scaife represents the interests of the English owners of copyright in the four pieces of music reprinted by Gilson and Ditson. (He was earlier responsible for convincing the U.S. Government that there is no necessity for engraving and printing music in America in order to secure copyright.)

The Association has decided to raise its subscription to ten guineas and to solicit additional contributions to a 'guarantee fund' to help prosecute the case. It is 'the duty of all publishers of music to subscribe liberally . . . The principle involved is perhaps the most important affecting our trade which has ever arisen'. After English publishers have announced their contributions other European music publishers will be applied to, 'as they are equally affected'.[94]

In an interview with the *Morning*, Mr. George Dixey amplifies some of the concerns. Though the U.S. Congress gave copyright to all works registered in Washington simultaneously with their English publication and later assured the Association that British works passing through Customs would not nullify that registration, some American publishers interpreted the rulings to mean that 'we had not the right to register in Washington unless we actually printed or engraved in the U.S.'

The intention of both parties in this proceeding, 'more or less friendly', is to settle this question finally. *L&PMTR*, p. 19

93. *It is the subject of two meetings on 8 and 29 April 1892, and the letter authorizing Mr. Scaife to proceed is included in the minutes for the latter (*Min. Bk*, 139). No copy of the original found. (See 'Missing Documents', Appendix pp. 143–4).*
The four pieces in question, printed in London, were granted copyright by the Librarian of Congress. Defendants reprinted the works and are now claiming Novello's copyright invalid because the works were produced in Britain.

94. *The letter of solicitation is recorded in the* Min. Bk. *at 9 April 1892.*

February 1893

The Music Travellers have held their fourth annual meeting and dinner, 30 December at the Bedford Head Hotel, Mr. F. Jefferys in the chair. *MO&MTR*, p. 304

September 1893

The *MO&MTR* reprints some of the 'London Correspondence of *The American Art Journal*', a report that the Music Publishers' Association is trying to secure a decision on the American copyright law, specifically, whether it is necessary to print music in America, or whether music is exempt from the manufacture clause covering 'books'.

The correspondent also goes to some length to explain that the right of performance is granted by the copyright owner to those who purchase a set of parts, but that the right is not extended to those who *borrow* sets of performance materials.

MO&MTR, p. 750

March 1894

Though the music publishing firm of Messrs. Broome was established in 1845, it is not so well-known as many others, dealing chiefly in 'cheap songs' as, for instance, Tarrant's *Old Sweet Greeting*, of which over 62,000 copies have been sold in fifteen months.

The present proprietor Broome has chronicled 210,000 customers with their names and addresses filling thirty-five volumes, to house which a strong room has just been built. He does his own printing. Collection and dispatch of orders requires two post office vans daily. *MO&MTR*, p. 388

15 May 1894

The Music Trades Section of the Chamber of Commerce has appointed a new chairman to fill the vacancy left by the resignation of Mr. James Hopkinson. At the annual meeting on 3 May, the choice fell on Mr. H. R. Clayton, one of the partners in Messrs. Novello, Ewer & Co., a barrister, and an acknowledged authority on the law of copyright. *L&PMTR*, p. 11

The present state of Canadian copyright is unsettling to British music publishers and is the subject of a lengthy discussion at the same meeting. The new Canadian Tariff Bill proposes a stop to the collection by Canadian Customs of royalties on foreign reprints of British copyright works for the benefit of the copyright holders. Canada wished to be released from the International Copyright Law between both England and America, 'no doubt with the object of again being able to import into their country cheap piratical reprints of foreign copyrights'. If Canada withdraws from the copyright arrangement, the United States will probably do the same.

As the *Musical Times* has pointed out, large sums of money are due from, and unpaid by, the Canadian authorities to British copyright owners.[95] *L&PMTR*, pp. 13, 15, 19, 29

95. *In one of the longest articles it ever devoted to copyright, the* Musical Times, *five years earlier in its issue for 1 Sept. 1889, provided a four-page history, analysis, and condemnation of Canada's copyright legislation—and motives—since 1850. (See also here under 15 Mar. 1895.)*

15 June 1894

'The British Government have concluded a Copyright Convention with Austria, and an Order in Council was officially gazetted' on 11 May.[96] A lengthy article summarizes the provisions which Mr. Clayton states are, on the whole, satisfactory. It is a pity that the Austrian Government have not joined the Copyright Union, however.

L&PMTR, pp. 13, 15

96. *The order is printed complete in the minutes of the Annual General Meeting of the MPA, 21 Jan. 1895* (Min. Bk., *183–84).*

15 July 1894

The Annual Report of the Music Publishers' Association includes, among 'miscellaneous' topics, a note that copies of the *Song Folio* are being offered for sale in Hull, and that the Association 'continues to issue large numbers of the notices respecting it, as well as others about unlawful copying and piracy'.[97]

L&PMTR, pp. 25, 27

97. *No copies of the original notices have been found. (See 'Missing Documents', Appendix, pp. 143–4).*

15 August 1894

The Secretary of the Music Publishers' Association has announced that the 'first round' in the two-year American Copyright fight has been decided in favour of the English publishers.[98] 'Pity it is that the American law courts cannot do their work a little more speedily and a good deal more cheaply' and that the German publishers have escaped from pecuniary contributions to the law costs.

L&PMTR, p. 15

98. *The text of the judgment, dated 1 Aug. 1894, is printed in* L&PMTR, *15 Sept. 1894 (p. 29).*

October 1984

'Since the teetotal movement commenced, it has been the means of creating very many wind and other bands. Lately, however, the employees of some of the great London breweries have caught the spirit of emulation, and have established wind bands also'.

MO&MTR, p. 52

15 October 1894

A summary of an article by Mrs. F. E. Thomas in the New York *Musical Courier* provides a comprehensive description of 'Music Publishing in France' and the ways in which it differs from the trade elsewhere.

The typical French publisher deals with three classes of composers and recompenses each in a different way. The work of an 'unknown' is printed and the publisher *sells* twenty-five to 100 copies to the composer at a reduced rate. If the work proves to be a success the publisher gains; if not, he loses little, and the composer has gained experience and copies for his friends.

For the known but not famous composer's work, the publisher bears the cost of printing and gives up to 100 copies without charge.

The price of works by the famous is fixed according to the supposed 'talent' value of the composer, a value exceedingly difficult, sometimes risky, to establish. 'Gounod might have offered a piece for 1,000 fr., Massenet the same for 500 fr., Reber for 300 fr.' It is not surprising that some inferior works come to be in greater demand than the splendid works of great artists. Last year twenty *cafe* concert songs—though already in vogue for as long as a dozen years—each sold over 50,000 copies.

The French publisher buys from the creator the copyright for all countries but rarely the performance rights, because of the complexities of bookkeeping; for example, the publisher might have a catalogue of over 40,000 pieces, as does the old firm of Richault & Cie.

For contemporary works, the copyright duration is for the life of the composer or proprietor plus fifty years.

French opera and theatre composers make the largest profits, first by the sale of their works to the publishers, then again through *droits d'auteur* which bring a royalty for each performance. Two protective societies collect these fees, one for works given at concerts (the Société des Auteurs, Compositeurs et Éditeurs de Musique, called the Souchon Society); the other for works performed in the theatres (the Société des Auteurs et Compositeurs, called the Roger Society). For his *Cinq mars*, for example, Gounod received 100,000 fr. for the copyright from his publisher, and when the opera is performed in France the Roger Society collects twelve per cent of each day's total receipts to divide among him, his librettist, and the society.

The society does not operate abroad; when performances occur there, a certain rental is paid to the publisher for the orchestral parts for a whole season, and this the publisher shares with the composer.

When only fragments of an opera are given, the Souchon Society gathers the proceeds and divides them among the three parties. In France alone, in only the past year, the Souchon Society has taken in over 1,000,000 fr., the Roger Society 2,000,000 (plus an extra 50,000 for Paris).

The benefits to composers have greatly increased. Forty years ago for his best comic opera Auber could get but 9,000 fr., 3,000 for each act, and the publisher sold outright—did not rent—the orchestral parts. Now it is the theatre director instead of the composer who is unfortunate, because he must rent the material, pay fees to two protective societies, as well as fees obligated to charity by the *Droit d'Assistance Publique.* The fees gathered from opera in France in 1893 for public charities amounted to more than 21,000,000 fr.

In the lobby of any Paris opera house, three gentlemen in evening dress wait to handle each ticket and to validate the receipts of the day's performances for the three organizations—the Souchon and Roger societies, and the *Assistance Publique.*

Aside from the payment to the composer, every published page of music costs the publisher about 5 fr. to 10 fr. for the plates and cover design. A five-page piano piece, therefore, would cost 25 to 50 fr., plus another 25 fr. for paper and printing of 100 copies. This low cost means that works in heavy demand are very profitable, as, for example, *Le Lac* by Nedermeyer to words by Lamartine, which for over forty years has regularly sold more than 3,000 copies a year. *L&PMTR*, pp. 31, 33

November 1894

Percy Ashdown, son and N.Y. representative of Edwin Ashdown (Ltd.), has opened a new store on East 14th St. in N.Y. Since opening the American branch in 1891 the stock has doubled and more room is needed to enhance contacts with out-of-town dealers, teachers and music students. In earlier years, many of the dealers visited by him or his travellers declared themselves overstocked with Ashdown publications, because ten years previously, when Ashdown (and other publishers) sold, as old paper, large quantities of 'unmerchantable' music, it was grabbed up by speculators for less then the cost of paper, then sold cheaply throughout Canada and the U.S. Drygoods stores could retail Ashdown print for less than dealers could buy it from Ashdown. *MO&MTR*, p. 121

15 January 1895

Litigation continues in the American Court of Appeals on the Novello vs. Ditson case and funds are still needed by the Music Publishers' Association to sustain the work. A very long letter from Mr. Dixey, Secretary of the Association [printed], responds to a letter from the German Music Publishers' Association on the subject of American copyright which appeared in both the *L&PMTR* for 15 Dec. 1894[99] and the *Musical Standard* for 1 Dec. 1894.

The Germans have declined to contribute to the funds being raised, their disinterest stemming from their belief that they enjoy copyright in America by virtue of a special treaty dated 15 Jan. 1892 [reprinted in full]. This treaty disposes of the requirement that works must be printed in America as a condition of obtaining copyright there. Dixey notes that the President of the U.S. 'satisfied himself that reciprocity already existed' between England and America at the time he signed the American Copyright Act of 1891; the treaty with Germany, therefore, 'merely supplied the omission which in the case of England never existed'. Both countries have the same benefits, and Dixey admonishes the Germans that everyone entitled to them must bear its burdens; the treaty only entitles one to the benefits of the American act; it gives no copyright. Germany's interests in the outcome of the appeal are identical to England's.[100] *L&PMTR*, pp. 17–18

99. *and discussed* ibid. *(pp. 11, 13, 29).*

100. *The exchange is also recorded in the* Min. Bk. *for the MPA meeting of 21 Jan. 1895 (p. 190) and its Annual Meeting, 14 June 1895* (Min. Bk., *196).*

15 February 1895

In a letter about the American copyright law, Dr. von Hase, of Breitkopf & Härtel, says that his firm's interest in the outcome of American legislation is not very great as its publications 'during the last two generations have been so thoroughly reprinted in America that the original editions could not be made deader than dead'. To guard its interests in the future, a modest branch house has been opened in New York, but the best means against reprinting is to publish only such works that are indigestible to the crowd, works that would 'occasion suffering to the reprinter', e.g., the large editions of Schütz, Palestrina, Bach, and Lassus.

He congratulates America for the new Act. 'According to my heretical views, America only now has joined the ranks of modern civilized countries', by breaking, with this act, 'the exclusion of foreign countries from the protection of internal law', granting this protection through the reciprocity clause. Now the U.S. must take another forward step and 'join the World's Union which was founded in Berne'. *L&PMTR*, p. 15

An editorial notes that von Hase has admitted some concern about the 'manufacture clause' in the American legislation. That the Germans 'should still decline to contribute to the necessary expenses, therefore, appears wretchedly mean'. *L&PMTR*, p. 17

15 March 1895

A bill to amend the Copyright Act in Canada has passed both Canadian houses and awaits the assent of Her Majesty. Information from the London Chamber of Commerce indicates how 'subversive' the changes would be, and the Chamber has circulated a petition addressed to the Marquis of Ripon, H.M. Secretary of State for the Colonies, urging that the royal assent be withheld.

In brief, the changes would give British authors copyright in Canada for twenty-eight years if they reprint and republish the work in Canada within one month of its original publication, but if the authors do not do so within one month, the Canadian Government may grant licenses to print editions, without the authors' consent, and collect ten per cent of the retail price from the licensee. The retail price, however, will be fixed by the publisher without consultation with the author. The bill does not say whether royalty is to be paid on copies printed or on copies sold.[101]

L&PMTR, p. 13

101. *Curiously, some six months earlier, in an article on 'Canadian Copyright' in its issue of 15 November 1894, the* Musical Times *notes that the Act 'was refused the royal assent', without noting that the first passage of the Act—and first refusal of the royal assent—took place in 1889!*

15 April 1895

The Oldham Music Trades Association has circulated a letter to ten leading music publishers wanting to know whether they are supplying professors at trade terms, and requesting that they restrict their business to *bona fide* members of the music trade.

Some answering letters are reprinted. Extracts from them include: '. . . our business is nearly all conducted with trade houses' (Chappell); '. . . we have very few accounts open with professors [and would prefer] that orders come through the trade' (Boosey); '. . . the complaints you refer to cannot in any way relate to us' (Robert Cocks); '. . . very few professional accounts are on our books, and . . . do not suppose that your circular is directed against us' (J. B. Cramer); '. . . for years past we have received circulars similar to [yours], and cannot offer any opinion in the matter' (Ashdown); '. . . [we allow discounts] only to actual members of the musical profession and trade. At the same time we would mention that we conduct our business in the manner we think best' (Novello); '. . . only *bona fide* members of the trade . . .' (Enoch); 'We beg to inform you that we *never* reply to circulars of the kind you sent us. We have the impression no one who knows our trade would have favoured us with it' (Schott). *L&PMTR*, p. 25

In a leading article in the next issue (p. 11), the editors review the problems of 'Supplying the Profession at Trade Prices', comment on the Oldham Association's circular, and the responses to it.

May 1895

Sydney Ashdown (in the U.S.) issues a pamphlet to allay publishers' fears that Canadian publishers may flood the U.S. and British markets with cheap editions. Importation and sales of unauthorized editions is prohibited by the copyright acts of those countries.

But he goes on to point out that three men in Toronto derive half of their income selling cheap Canadian reprints of American copyright works.[102] He estimates there are £15,000 sterling worth of American reprints presently in England. Frequently half of a gathering of music that he has been asked to bind infringes his own copyrights. Canadian and American border dealers keep reprints of copyrights from the other country to sell cheaply to those who cross the border. *MO&MTR*, p. 523

102. *An article in* L&PMTR *several years later (15 June 1898, p. 28) notes that the U.S. Congress will take action to check this illegal traffic which 'is flooding American cities with copies of songs supposed to be protected by copyright'. The assistant superintendent of mails in Buffalo writes that while his department was watching the Canadian mails, Canadian publishers sent illegal copies across the border outside the mail, then posted them in Buffalo. 'Yesterday we held several hundred parcels'.*

June 1895

The friction which has existed between publishers, 'wholesalers', and music dealers results in a circular [reprinted) signed by twenty-three distinguished publishers, among them Augener, Chappell, Cocks & Co., Ricordi, and Schott. Accusing dealers of underselling to the trade their copyrighted publications, they will in the future 'execute no journey orders for any dealers who adopt this

103. *Printed earlier in* L&PMTR, *15 May 1895 (p. 23) and discussed in a leading article (p. 11). No copies of the circular found. (See 'Missing Documents', Appendix, pp. 143–4).*

method of business'.[103]

A 'counterblast' issued by Messrs. George & Co. of Tottenham Court Road questions the publishers' motives: 'Why should the publishers be so anxious to see the wholesaler make an enormous [he means conventional!] profit ... Why, then, should not the buyer be permitted to sell at whatever price he likes?' Publishers, he says, force dealers to take many novelties that do not sell; they are 'the publishers' heaven-provided rubbish pit'. Publishers want to continue trading directly with *both* wholesaler and dealer, offering the same discount to each. If the wholesaler must then sell to the dealer at retail prices, the dealer cannot profit. Nor can any dealer hope to lay in sufficient stock to meet all requirements. The same publishers are undercutting the dealers by taking orders from 'those who supply the public direct at less than a third: drapers, provision dealers, stores and such like'. Publishers, while indignant at finding their own prints at a wholesalers, will use that same wholesaler to secure other publishers' prints at reduced prices.[104]

MO&MTR, pp. 595–96

104. *Printed* ibid. *(pp. 23,25) under the caption, 'To the retail music trade. Are you to be made to pay a third for all your collecting?'*

Another circular signed by fourteen wholesalers, including Hart & Co., Morley and Son, W. H. Broome, and H. Wilcock, notes that most of the publishers signing the circular sell to schools on better terms than those offered the trade and 'take "professionals" at their own valuation'. The circular asks dealers to send responses to six questions, among which are: 1) 'Will you undertake to sell sheet music . . . at less than one third'; not to assist those of the trade who do; to consider raising the retail price from 4d. to 1s. 6½; to create an association, dues at 5s. per annum.[105] *MO&MTR*, p. 596

105. *Another circular of which no original has been found. (See 'Missing Documents', Appendix, pp. 143–4).*

W. Phillips of Tunbridge Wells points out that since the retail price was reduced to one-third [sold to the public at the 'trade price', one-third off the marked price] sales have increased and publishers have reaped the entire benefit; the loss has fallen upon the retail dealers.[106] *MO&MTR*, pp. 597–98

106. *Discussed in* L&PMTR, *15 May 1895 (p. 11) and reprinted (pp. 21, 23).*

Mr. George, in another lengthy letter, asserts the need for and the legitimate standing of collecting houses. Publishers should not be expected to reduce their justifiable terms, but 'having got their price, they should be satisfied, and not expect it twice over'. Proposed remedy: Let the publishers' price be, say, 1s., the wholesalers' 1s. 2d., the retailer to sell at 1s. 4d., the essence of it that the publisher maintain a fixed price to the wholesaler. Once more the publishers' surfeit of novelties is attacked: 'An order without novelties the publishers treat as a deadly insult'. *MO&MTR*, p. 598

A letter from G. Dixey of the Music Publishers' Association reports that in the Novello & Co. vs. Oliver Ditson case heard by the Boston Court of Appeals, the judgment is that a 'music composition is not a "book" within the manufacturing clause of the American Copyright Act of 1891 . . .' A musical composition, therefore, need not be printed in America as a condition of obtaining American copyright.[107] *MO&MTR*, p. 598

July 1895

In another long letter, three columns in length, Mr. E. George, the wholesaler, once more states his feelings about the publishers' circular to collecting houses [*see* June 1895]. He is supported fully in another long letter from James W. Hime of Fulham Road.[108] *MO&MTR*, pp. 670–74

August 1895

'Big Drum', a small provincial dealer, supports Mr. George's arguments against the publishers who 'condescendingly descend to supply you at wholesale prices' twice a year, when their traveller calls, but at retail every other day. Publishers have ruined the trade, supplying anyone at wholesale prices over the counter, instead of giving the wholesale terms to dealers only. If he was to stock what the travellers think he ought, 'so as to have everything likely to be asked for—I should want our local town hall and parish church to hold it . . . I say to Messrs. George and others, more power to your elbow'. *MO&MTR*, p. 733

15 August 1895

The gross total of imports of musical instruments from abroad in 1893 was £942,989. The gross total of musical instruments exported was £198,248. Grand total of exports and imports, therefore, £1,141,237. *L&PMTR*, p. 21

October 1895

M.P. writes to take the side of the publishers against the collecting houses who, he says, cut prices. He proposes a close association of dealers and publishers whose members would be pledged to a scale of trade terms worked out jointly. The agreement would include the terms upon which retail traders would be supplied between journey orders.

The proposed association and trade terms would effectively eliminate the wholesalers.[109]

Another writer tries to calm the controversy by suggesting an association of all—publishers, wholesalers, and dealers—based on

107. *The original court action, a test case brought on behalf of the Music Publishers' Association, is fully reported in the* Musical News, *Sept. 1894 (p. 201). The same report indicates that this appeal was planned and that British publishers subscribed a total of £1000 for both cases. A letter from Mr. Dixey about the decision in the first case is reported in the* News, *August 1894, another letter, about the decision in the appeal, 4 May 1895.*

Under the heading, 'The American Copyright Case—Victory of the British Publishers', L&PMTR, *15 May 1895 (pp. 17–18) reprints verbatim from the New York* Musical Courier *the decision of the Circuit Court and the Appellate Court on 25 April upholding the Circuit Court's first judgement (p. 13). The same text is also reprinted in* Musical Times, *1 June 1895 (pp. 374–75), and in a brief paragraph a month later,* The Times *reports that the defendants have decided not to appeal to the Supreme Court. The litigation, therefore, is finally closed.*

The case was discussed at every meeting (eight in all) of the MPA from June of 1895 to 3 June 1896.

108. *Hime's letter is also printed in full in the* L&PMTR *for 15 June 1895 (pp. 25, 27).*

109. *Another long letter from M.P. expressing the same opinions appears in* L&PMTR, *15 Sept. 1895 (p. 21), whose editor points out that 'M.P.' is not a Member of Parliament but a 'name very famous in the music publishing world'.*

the 'equitable features of co-operation on what is known as the Rochdale principle'. *MO&MTR*, p. 51

15 October 1895

The Secretary of the Music Publishers' Association announces that the offices of the Association and those of the Anglo-Canadian Music Publishers' Association have been moved to 9, Air Street, about which the editor comments: 'It is so long since we have heard from the secretary in question that his existence had almost been forgotten. In the early days of the Association', it was 'always *en evidence*'. *L&PMTR*, p. 33

November 1895

'Not an M.P.' offers a four-column retort to M.P.'s article the previous month, beginning: 'There is an inner and an outer aspect to every occupation in life'. From this the writer proceeds to excoriate the publishers' action, to chide those who propose that only 'meritorious' music be published and sold (it is success and what sells that counts), to demand that the publishers maintain a fixed price for the trade, to insist that collecting houses are essential if the retailer is to maintain a sellable range of stock, and to urge the publishers to recant their 'egregious blunder', the circular.
MO&MTR, p. 121

A 'London Dealer' concurs with those who criticize the tenets of 'M.P.' [Oct. 1895] and discusses at length various pricing procedures, both those presently in effect, and those proposed in the course of this controversy. If a retail trade association is needed, it is needed 'not for leaguing with the publishers against the collectors but for combining amongst ourselves to exact better terms and conditions from the publishers'. *MO&MTR*, p. 123

15 November 1895

At the congress of the International and Artistic Association at Dresden, vain attempts are made to persuade German and British publishers to enter upon the French system of *petits droits*. Herr Boch, a music publisher speaks for the system (his speech is reprinted in an English translation from the New York *Musical Courier*). Dr. von Hase, head of Breitkopf & Härtel, speaks in opposition.

In the reporter's opinion, the British system of performing rights is probably the best. Any British composer who thinks otherwise, however, 'can conserve all his performing rights by making an announcement to that effect on the title-page', but his songs will 'probably remain unsung'. *L&PMTR*, pp. 12–13

15 March 1896

The Metropolitan Musicsellers Association, 'formed after a lengthy correspondence in our columns last year', banquetted on 13 February. Its membership includes seventy firms. In the course of the banquet it was mentioned that Messrs. Orsborn, Patey & Willis, Mathias & Strickland, and Robert Cocks & Co. 'have made concessions as to terms for collecting. Messrs. Metzler may do so soon, and it is hoped that other publishers will do likewise.'

L&PMTR, p. 33

1 April 1896

A draft of a new American copyright bill submitted to the U.S. Congress by Mr. Treloar on 13 Feb. 1896 will, if passed, become law on 1 July. Some of its provisions, and some of the ambiguities especially affecting the British trade, are discussed by Edward Cutler, Q.C., in a leading article.[110] Of all the possible changes, the most significant may involve that of reciprocity. Under the Act of 1891 [see April 1891], non-Americans of a state which confers reciprocal benefits are entitled to copyright in the U.S., and though the new bill does not explicitly revoke that benefit, it does not explicitly reaffirm it, either. There is reason to fear it might vacate the decisions regarding the so-called 'manufacture clause' in the Novello vs. Ditson case by extending reciprocity to authors and proprietors 'provided they comply with the formalities', one of those being the delivery of two copies of a musical composition printed from type, engraved plates, or transfers *made in the U.S.*. In effect, this would reinstitute that 'manufacture clause', and is a matter for grave concern.

Other provisions of the bill raise no such concerns. Among them are these: 1) minimum penalty of $100 for unlawful performance of dramatic or operatic compositions; 2) term of copyright changed from twenty-eight years with renewal for fourteen, to a term of forty years, renewable for twenty; 3) importation of piratical matter is now a misdemeanor; 4) packages suspected of containing piratical matter may be inspected by postal or custom officials; and 5) notice of claim to copyright must appear on each work.

Musical Times, pp. 225–26

110. *Cutler, an expert on copyright matters, later published* A Manual of Musical Copyright Law; for the Use of Music Publishers and Artists. *London: Simpkin, Marshall [etc.], 1905.*

In a letter reprinted in this same issue, Henry R. Clayton of the MPA vehemently attacks the proposed bill, referring at length to the reciprocity established in the Act of 1891 and to the elimination of the 'manufacture clause' in the Novello vs. Ditson case. He finds the bill 'replete with doubts and ambiguities, not to say absurdities ... The rights of foreigners are in a state of delightful doubt'.

Musical Times, p. 268

May 1896

[Reprinted from the N.Y. *Musical Courier*] Sebastian Schlesinger in Paris writes about 'Publishers and Vocalists', responding to a letter from the publisher Robert Cocks (printed under the caption, 'High Class Songs') in which Cocks claims it does not pay to publish good songs; the public does not appreciate them, and vocalists will not sing them without being paid for doing so when, in fact, they should do so 'for the love of their art'.

Schlesinger replies to Cocks, blaming the publishers: 'England [is] the only country to my knowledge, where publishers [pay] vocalists for singing their publications ... They pay the highest premium for singing the worst songs ... The class of songs sung in England would not be tolerated in America'.

Mr. Cocks responds: 'We quite agree with what you say. English publishers are greatly to blame for the state of things'. As about the last house to pay vocalists, Cocks & Co., he says, were obliged to do so in self-defence. Cocks and Schlesinger agree that vocalists should decline to sing trashy songs, even for pay.

MO&MTR, p. 555

8 August 1896

'The Profit of Popular Songs!' Mr. George Maywood (née Schleiffarth), who lives in the United States, says that he has composed 15,000 pieces. The *Musical Standard* editor seems dubious, estimating that in a career of twenty years that would mean 535 pieces a year or one and one-third pieces each day—not counting Sundays. Mr. Maywood concedes that some of his popular songs have brought him only £200. *Musical Standard, Illus. Ser.*, p. 68

15 August 1896

Taking advantage of the presence of 'dealers up for the Music Trades Exhibition at the Agricultural Hall', a meeting is called to get publishers and dealers together to discuss trade prices of sheet music. Forty provincial dealers attend, no publishers, which is unfortunate, for nothing practical will be achieved until they are brought face to face. 'It is quite obvious that the publishers are keeping well together ...' and at the present time 'seem to have their knife chiefly into the collecting houses'.[111]

The dealers have undoubted matters for complaint: the higher cost for a song on re-order than when bought from a traveller; price cutting by other dealers and the Stores; and publishers selling at discounts to schools *L&PMTR*, pp. 11, 13

111. *There is nothing in the MPA* Min. Bk. *about this meeting. The absence of* all *of the publishers from it indicates a private and informal, but very effective, arrangement.*

15 September 1896

The question of discounts on sheet music remains one that the dealers must settle with the publishers direct. Those who keep stocks are now obliged to buy copyright music at practically the same price they sell, i.e., at one-third or thereabouts. When a traveller calls, dealers can purchase at a lower price, if novelties are accepted. 'There is no branch of the trade in which cutting is so actively practiced.' The Stores, which only obtain music to order, supply at a discount. 'Dealers who stock should have the stuff at cheaper prices'. *L&PMTR*, p. 15

October 1896

'One Who has Tried', apparently a country musicseller, recounts his experiences with publishers' travellers. Having stated his wishes, he is reminded by the traveller that, 'We cannot execute your order unless you take "novelties" in proportion'. He is shown a two-page list, those on one side 'seven copies for 6s., while on the other they are 8s.', an extra 2s. for royalties (the publisher must pay its composers 4d. per copy). The musicseller asks if *he* is not the one who is paying the royalties—and a little more. The traveller points out that the publishers charge only an average of 1s. for ordinary stock and 8d. for novelties, the dealer to choose how many he wants of the former, the publisher to dictate how many of the latter he must buy. The dealer calculates that for every 4d. he makes on ordinary stock he will 'probably lose 6d. by having so much dead stuff in the shape of novelties'. Lost, 2d. Traveller suggests that he 'push the novelties'.

The dealer complies. Having pushed several novelties with success, he reorders, assuming that the price will be 8d. per copy, as the week before. Not so. The publisher says the pieces are now very popular, not novelties, that when the traveller returns in three months the dealer can buy all he wants of those titles at the ordinary stock price of 10½d. (or if royalties, 1s. 2d.) provided he buys another batch of novelties.

Dealer insists he wants the copies now, but the publisher will do so only at the retail price, 1s. 4d. Dealer's profit on this transaction, 2½d. per piece.

Dealer, however, accepts and works very hard for several months. When the traveller next calls he has a large order ready. After an unduly long wait for delivery, instead of the music the publisher sends a letter asking why he has submitted such a large order and demanding: 'Are you supplying the trade?'

MO&MTR, p. 53

15 November 1896

The importation of foreign copyrights is greatly affected by the important appeal case of Pitts vs. George & Co., having to do with the question whether 'it was lawful to import into this country music by foreigners copyright here, but printed in the town where the work was first published'. The subject is Raff's *La Fileuse*, now the copyright in England of Messrs. Pitts. Messrs. George & Co., well-known collectors to the trade, imported a number of copies printed in Leipzig where it was first published, under the provisions of Section 10 of the International Copyright Act of 1844.

At the initial trial, Justice Kekewich held for the defendant's right to import the piece. The Court of Appeal, though only by a majority, upset this judgement; 'at the present time, therefore, it is two on one side against two on the other'. The case ought to go to the House of Lords, but the judgment stands that 'when foreign music has been copyrighted in England, it is unlawful for any one, without the consent of the copyright holder, to import copies of such music printed abroad'. *L&PMTR*, pp. 14, 27

2 January 1897

'The Association for the Suppression of Street Noises has issued several leaflets, the most striking of which is one informing householders that organ grinders and other "so-called" street musicians are bound to remove from the neighbourhood, under penalty of fine or imprisonment and that they may be given into custody if they persist . . .'[112] *Musical News*, p. 5

112. *The streets of nineteenth century London were heavily populated by all sorts of street 'musicians', and there was constant talk of laws needed to suppress 'street music'—all duly reported over a period of many years in the journals and newspapers. Much earlier, in its third issue of 27 March 1891, the* Musical News *had commented (pp. 69–70) on a new 'Street Music Bill' to take care of the 'prowling German brass bands' and the 'strident piano-organs' which 'make the day hideous and night unendurable'.*

April 1897

An unusual case of 'infringement' is heard in Lambeth County Court. The plaintiff, Mrs. R. V. Simons (known as Blanch Harcourt) decided to return to the music hall stage and contracted with a composer, Mr. McGlennon, to provide her something 'new'. In June she rehearsed two new songs with him, one of them *That's not my Style*, whose copyright she agreed to purchase. In December, in a costume especially made for the piece, she presented it for the first time at the Peckham Theatre of Varieties, but before she was halfway through the first verse, was challenged for singing another lady's (a Miss Le Roy's) song—a great offence against music hall traditions. Assured by Miss Le Roy that she had the assignment of the song, the proprietor would not let Mrs. Simons continue and declined to give her a return engagement until the matter is settled.

The case grows more and more complex as the author of the text, a Mr. Horncastle, and another composer, Mr. Atkins, from whom Miss Le Roy secured her assignment, are drawn into the case. Eventually the jury finds for Mrs. Simons, plaintiff, who is awarded £10 by the judge. *MO&MTR*, p. 486

July 1897

A correspondent of the *Musical News* reports that the music for a children's demonstration in connection with the Queen's recent visit to Sheffield was issued and circulated as 'arranged by Dr.

Henry Coward', without acknowledgement on the copies that it was based on Sir Michael Costa's arrangement owned by Messrs. Novello. The firm took steps to set the matter right which involved obliterating Dr. Coward's name and substituting 'By the kind permission of Novello, Ewer & Co., Costa's Arrangement' on something like 30,000 copies!

A lengthy letter of explanation from Novello & Co. responds to the questions which have, naturally, arisen, offering proof that the Coward arrangement was based heavily on Costa, and more impor tantly, that the circulation of 30,000 copies without disclosure of Novello's ownership was a far greater trespass—in effect, 'an advertisement to the world at large that the owner has no copyright interest in his own property'. Indeed, within a few days, a copy of the illegal printing arrived at Novello's London office with an innocent request for an estimate of their cost of reproducing several thousand copies!

In explaining why Coward's arrangement remains essentially Costa's—and therefore Novello's—despite some alterations, the firm states that 'Costa not only conceived and planned certain characteristics of his own, but he arranged them in a certain defined order. His arrangement *does not depend* upon any of those characteristics; it *consists* of the whole of them. No one else may do as he did. Each one of his characteristics may or may not of itself be sufficient to entitle him to monopolise it; but united they must stand as Costa's, and no one else's'.

MO&MTR, p. 702

15 July 1897

'A new Copyright Amendment Bill has been introduced into the House of Lords by Lord Monkswell . . . It is an "amending" rather than a "codifying" Bill, more or less founded on the representations of the Royal Commission on Copyright of 1878'.

Musical News, p. 13

October 1897

The publishers Francis, Day & Hunter, acting with Messrs. Sheard & Co., have obtained an injunction against the reprinters of a number of their copyrighted songs, including one of Francis & Day's best, *Soldiers of the Queen*, by Leslie Stuart. Just before the injunction was obtained, some 2,000 copies of the pirated edition were found stacked up ready for delivery. All copies have now been burned, the plates broken and melted down. Messrs. Ricordi, too, have captured the pirate of the popular song, Pinsuti's *Queen of the Earth*, 'and the erstwhile paper stainer is now on the stool of repentance'.

MO&MTR, pp. 59–60

January 1898

The successes of several publishers in combatting pirates by means of injunction during the latter half of 1897 is noted, but the steady increase in piratical activities brings some of the principal music publishers together for a meeting on 14 December 1897. The circular[113] announcing the meeting points out that two publishers have already obtained protection other than that granted by the Copyright Act and suggests that, with concerted action, some ways of checking the illegal traffic might be found until a short act of Parliament can be passed which would give music publishers 'the same rights as are given to owners of prints, photographs, &c.—i.e., to seize all illegal reprints'.

113. *No copy of the original document found. (See 'Misssing Documents', Appendix, pp. 143–4).*

Mr. Ashdown chairs the meeting. Mr. Enoch declares that what is needed is a bill like the Fine Arts Bill, but these take a long time to pass. A truculent Mr. Orsborn says that his solicitor has found a way to put an end to the pirates, that he advises any gentleman who wants to know that method to see him. Mr. Boosey wonders whether they should 'take the matter into their own hands'. Mr. Enoch thinks they should fight as a body for what Mr. Orsborn has done. Mr. Orsborn recommends that 'when they see a man with a stall, to go through the music and take the pirated copies away'. Mr. Boosey proposes that the Music Publishers' Association work to get a bill through the House of Commons that would allow publishers to deal in a summary way with infringements. Motion carries. Mr. Sheard says publishers should make it known that 'any piracy will be dealt with by the association'. On that threatening note, meeting adjourns.[114] *MO&MTR*, p. 269

114. *This air of truculence is not, however, reflected or recorded in the official minutes for this meeting (*Min. Bk.*, 231–[34])!*

March 1898

The magnitude of the problem with pirates is implicit in statements made by Mr. Henry Davey at a meeting of Tonic-sol-fa Society where he estimates that some 20 million pieces of music are being sold in England each year. He describes how he arrived at that figure. Astonishing as it is, he points out that it does not include the illegal reprints of pirates. *MO&MTR*, p. 417

April 1898

The vigorous prosecution of piratic music publishers by several American houses—most notably John Church Co. in the case of its Sousa marches—has drawn much comment in England. Hawkers of copyrights are becoming a nuisance, and the summary methods employed by Mr. Orsborn ('a man of mettle') have gained wide approval.

To stop the piratical sale of Piccolomini's *Whisper, and I Shall Hear* by the peripatetic musicsellers of the gutter, Mr. Orsborn ascertained the name of the printer of the two pirated editions, applied for and was granted an injunction, 'sailed out into the streets', and seized some 500 copies of the song. Learning that a large stock of the edition was concealed in a public house, he 'and his merry men' went there and after some trouble managed to capture 2,000 more copies.[115]

115. *This 'remedy, which we proposed some time ago', is reported in the* L&PMTR, *15 Mar. 1898 (p. 13).*

In the same article the *MO&MTR* offers an elaborate description of Lord Monkswell's introduction of a short bill; a report on the Society of Authors-sponsored Copyright Amendment Bill; the status of several other pieces of copyright legislation, with their amendments, in the various committees of the two houses; and identifies the virtues of a so-called Consolidation Bill. With little chance that such a comprehensive new bill will be passed soon, however, the *MO&MTR* reports that the 'half loaf', Lord Monkswell's short bill, is strongly favoured by music publishers.[116]

116. *A discussion of several of its provisions appears in the* Musical News, *31 July 1897 (pp. 97–98).*

A memorial for Sir Albert Rollitt, M.P., is reprinted. It was sent to the House Secretary on behalf of three of the publishing trade sections of the London Chamber of Commerce and covers seven points: 1) the short bill just introduced is in behalf of the lawful owners of copyrights; 2) those owners are suffering at the hands of the pirates who, in effect, confiscate copyrights. 3) Pirates are difficult to apprehend, because their reprints bear no names or addresses, or display fictitious names and addresses. Piracies are sold house to house by hawkers who are lost sight of beforc, under the present law, a summons can be secured. An elaborate, secret system of distribution confounds the rightful owners and the law. Points 4) and 5) add details and emphasis: provisions of the present laws are inadequate and complicated, because publishers must proceed by summons, because there is no means of enforcing an order to deliver illegal copies and because no power is given to enter a home to search for those copies. Finally, the memorial asks the legislature to effect the recommendations of the Royal Commission on Copyright of 1878: grant the power to seize piracies 'without warrant by any peace officer under the orders and responsibility of the proprietor of the copyright'.[117]

117. *Reprinted, with commentary, in* L&PMTR, *15 Mar. 1895 (pp. 13, 15).*

Music publishers indicate unanimous support for the memorial. 'So far as they are concerned, *the trouble has originated within the last eight months* [emphasis supplied]. The increase in deliberate piracy and systematic selling of illegal reprints amounts to an organized conspiracy'. *MO&MTR*, pp. 483–84

July 1898

A select committee of the House of Lords hears testimony about the bills introduced by Lords Herschell and Monkswell. Mr. Clayton of Novello, Chairman of the Musical Trades Section[118] the London Chamber of Commerce, sets forth some grievances. Publishers want the limiting words, 'for sale or hire', in the law regard-

118. *Throughout the years, this was variously called the Music Trades Section, the Music Publishers' Section, and the Music Publishers' Sub-Section in the journals and newspapers, and also in the MPA* Min. Bk.

ing imported music either eliminated or expanded to include private use. They wish to prevent the importation of German publications by collecting firms which cannot be 'bound' by English publishers, and they want the 'power to deal with the barrel organs which appropriate copyright tunes'. They ask that a clause be inserted into the law providing that boys in the street selling pirated music, after being warned by a constable, should be guilty of an indictable misdemeanor.[119] *MO&MTR*, p. 707

119. *H. Reginald Clayton's representations to the committee are also reported fully in the* Musical News, *25 June 1898 (pp. 615–16), and verbatim in* L&PMTR, *15 May 1898 (pp. 13, 15, 17).*

15 July 1898

The 4th Annual Meeting of the Music Publishers' Association of the U.S. was held in New York on 14 June. About 100 firms are represented. Speeches and discussions centre around the establishment of fixed rates of discount, improving the present copyright laws, the rights of makers of mechanical instruments to use copyright pieces, and the evils of price-cutting. *L&PMTR*, p. 30

August 1898

In an article, 'A Year's Output of Music', the writer, 'Rex', who prepares the 'New Issues' columns for the *MO&MTR*, provides more data about the size of the music publishing industry in which the pirates are operating. He estimates that a 'representative concern' issues twenty to thirty compositions each month. Since there are a score of such concerns in London alone, the annual output there must be well over 5,000 works. 'Small fry' publishers issue at least ten pieces a month, and taking into account London 'small fry' and provincial firms, the total must be about 25,000 novelties a year. He arrives at a grand total of 40,000 titles a year.

Rex states that no publisher will print fewer than 200 copies of each work, so the annual result is 'not far short of eight and a half million copies of new music thrown upon the market by British publishers alone'. *MO&MTR*, p. 772

15 September 1898

Towards the end of the session of Parliament, the Copyright Committee 'suddenly collapsed'. Lord Herschel is going to the U.S., and the Committee has come to the conclusion that it is too late to reorganize. Nothing can be done until Parliament meets again in February. Though Mr. Clayton and Mr. Cutler have both given much valuable evidence to the Committee, more important information to come, namely about the wholesale distribution of pirated reprints. Lord Herschel's Copyright Bill will have to be reintroduced. 'If Parliament would spare an evening from pure politics', to deal with important matters, 'it would be doing useful work'. *L&PMTR*, p. 17

25 March 1899

An advertisement states: 'The Music Publishing Association . . . has been formed to publish music for Composers on such terms that the Composer will receive the full benefit of any financial reward (less a small commission) . . . which is not the case with the existing system of . . . the present publishing houses, who take nearly all the financial benefits'. Temporary offices are at 4, Laureldale Buildings, Aldersgate St. *Musical News*, p. 309

In an earlier comment on the scheme (11 March 1899) the *Musical News* reports that 'Thematic Lists' of available works of young composers will be widely circulated (to 16,000 church organists, for example) and that 'the plates will be the property of the composers. The scheme deserves to succeed'. *Musical News*, p. 218

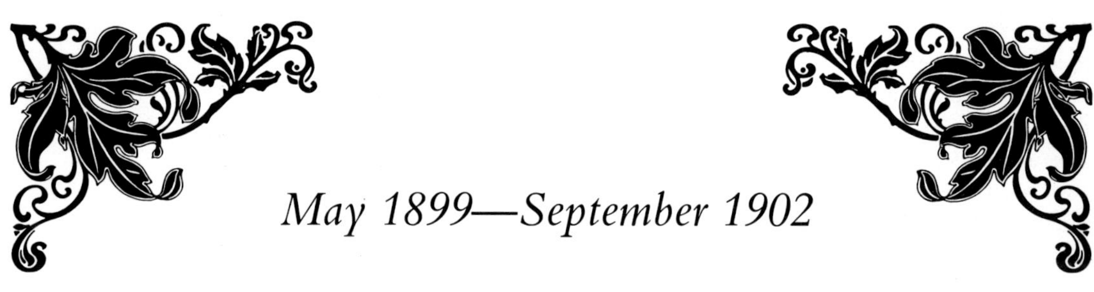

May 1899—September 1902

Boosey vs. Whight. An important case commences.

Lord Monkswell's Select Committee takes testimony on copyright and the vexing Aeolian dilemma.

Mr. Broome (he of the 210,000 customers) tells how quickly he can publish a piece of music.

Leslie Stuart reports that 100,000 illegal copies of his works have been produced by the pirates.

Copyright registration, fees, and library deposits prompt concern.

Worry about Clause 6 of the Berne Convention persists.

The Fourth International Congress of Publishers in Leipzig hears papers by British music publishers.

Dealers continue to complain about publishers' practices.

Doggerel invades the MO&MTR.

Publishers take the law (some of it) into their own hands.

A Musical Copyright Association forms.

A 'pirate's ship' is 'overhauled'.

Some hawkers cry 'foul', but the judge says they will 'have to stand the racket'.

May 1899

Boosey vs. Whight.[120] Messrs. Boosey seek to restrain Whight from selling perforated rolls of paper that reproduce, on an instrument called the Aeolian, three of Boosey's more popular songs. Boosey contends that the rolls are copies, in a different notation, of the sheets published by them. Defendants claim the rolls are merely part of the machinery for producing sounds. Justice Stirling finds for the defendants on this point, but because words have been added to the rolls indicating 'pace and expression at and with which the said music ought to be played', and because these words are taken from Boosey's published sheets, defendants are beyond their legal rights—this was 'flat as a burglary'—and they are restrained from publishing the rolls. [From the *Daily Telegraph*][121]

MO&MTR, p. 563

June 1899

Lord Monkswell's Select Committee sits on 8 May[122] to hear testimony about the transfer of copyrighted music onto perforated rolls in 'a sort of secret language', for playing on instruments such as the Aeolian. The decision of Justice Stirling in the Boosey vs. Whight case is acknowledged but disputed and a plea is made to extend copyright protection to paper rolls.

Further testimony turns on different wordings in the Customs Act and the copyright law. The Customs Act allows seizure of certain copies of works coming from abroad but does not define what pirated copies are. The representatives of the Copyright Association wish to have inserted an extended definition of piracy so that copies printed abroad—even lawfully—cannot be introduced into England.

Viscount Knutsford says he enjoys the Aeolian in his bedroom and does not understand how thwarting the production of perforated rolls by extending the copyright protection on printed music to the rolls will aid the composer. 'I should not purchase any of his music [in print] in any case, and I could not read it if I did'. The publishers' representatives claim no desire to halt the sale of Aeolians but want only royalties to be paid for the music used.

Mr. David Day, of Francis, Day & Hunter, asks that the penalty for hawking private books presently in the Copyright Bill embody a clause providing the power to search for and seize unlawful copies—a clause already in the Artistic Copyright Bill covering prints, and the like. Pirated songs are selling widely for 2d. Registration of titles would help. In America, he notes, registration costs one dollar, a register is published weekly, and nonregistration forfeits copyright. Stopping piracy with current laws requiring publishers to serve injunctions is too costly, slow, and troublesome.

MO&MTR, p. 630

120. *An account of this case before judgment was reached—condensed from* The Times *of 22 and 23 Feb.—is printed in the* L&PMTR *for 15 Mar. 1898 (p. 29), and in the* Musical News *16 (11 Mar. 1899): 247–48). Another article in the* MO&MTR *for 15 May 1899 (p. 11) summarizes the issues and the judgment, and the judgment itself is reprinted (pp. 17–18) in the* Musical News *17 (30 Dec. 1899): 592–93.*

The problem is noted in the minutes for meetings of MPA Committee as early as 2 Feb. 1898. The Secretary reported that he had written the Aeolian Organ & Automatic Pianoforte Co. (Messrs. Whight & Co.) noting that their catalogue contained copyright items being infringed. 'The results of numerous letters and interviews had been an offer from Messrs. G. Whight & Co. to pay a royalty under certain conditions' (Min. Bk., *235). The offer is again recorded in the minutes for 29 June 1898* (Min. Book., *241), but it was resolved at 'a meeting of members [seven: Enoch, Morley, Augener, Boosey, Ashdown, Hammond and Ricordi] to take proceedings against Messrs. Whight'. At the 27 April 1899 meeting it was decided to take the unsuccessful case to the Court of Appeal, and a guarantee fund was set up.*

121. *On appeal, in December 1899, this was overturned: 'the sheet of paper so perforated was not a copy of the sheet of music . . .' and furthermore, '. . . the printed directions . . . as to time and expression did not constitute an infringement'.*

This decision in the Court of Appeal was the basis for a later one in an important case in 1907, Newark vs. National Phonograph Co. Plaintiff, registered owner of the song, The Paralytic Hotel *charged the Company with making and selling phonograph recordings of the piece, rendering it valueless to him for singing in music halls. Defendants successfully used the arguments of the Boosey vs. Whight case.*

Quotations and summary here are from Albert A. Strong's Dramatic and Musical Law, *3d ed., pp. 113–14 (London: 'The Era', 1910).*

Dr. Rea's remarks about cheap music are reported: 'The whole of Beethoven's thirty-eight sonatas, for example, can now be purchased for half the price formerly demanded for one of these immortal compositions'. As prices have gone down quality has gone up. Old, expensive editions from pewter plates were half illegible and full of mistakes. New editions from movable type are clear, free of errors, carefully edited, include hints for performance and historical information on the piece and the composer.

Bowerman & Co. is awarded an injunction restraining Augener & Co. from selling copies of Steingräber editions of classical compositions for which Bowerman & Co. hold the British copyrights.[123] *MO&MTR*, p. 637

July 1899

The Select Committee continues its hearings. Professor Mayor from the University of Toronto argues for the protection of works published in Canada by legal prohibition of a copy of the same work printed elsewhere in the U.K. and imported into Canada. All such copies should be deemed pirated copies.

Mr. Moul, of the Society of Authors, Composers, and Music Publishers of France worries about protecting the rights of authors of lyric texts and wishes to have a phrase inserted to make their protection more explicit.

Mr. Cutler suggests a clause preventing the taking down of improvisations and publishing them without authority. He notes his own taking down of improvised fugues of Guilmant. He also supports the decision of the Court of First Instance in the Aeolian case.[124] *MO&MTR*, p. 702

At a meeting of the Music Publishers Section of the London Chamber of Commerce, Mr. Henry Clayton (Novello, Ewer & Co.) in the chair, recounts activities on the Copyright Bill since the last meeting, noting that he, himself, testified for about four and one-half hours before the special committee of the House of Lords.

A special resolution passes commending Mr. Clayton for his actions promoting the interest of the publishers.

MO&MTR, p. 703

15 July 1899

The Music Publishers Section of the London Chamber of Commerce is insulted because it has been informed that the British music publishers are not eligible to be present at the International Congress of Music Publishers. A protest, 'in dignified terms', is 'amply justified'. *L&PMTR*, p. 19

122. *It had, in fact, been meeting for some weeks past, dealing with a variety of questions relating to literary and artistic copyright. Committee hearings, extensively reported in* L&PMTR, *15 June 1899 (pp. 23–29), dealt with simultaneous publications in and out of the Kingdom, dramatic and musical copyright, mechanical musical instruments, piracy of popular songs, foreign musical performing rights in England. Some of the testimony of David Day, of J. M. Glover, Director of Music at the Drury Lane, and of Edward Cutler, Q.C., is also printed in the* Musical News *16 (20 May 1899): 534.*

123. L&PMTR, *15 June 1899 (p. 27).*

124. *Vigorous protests from Novello & Co. in a letter to* The Standard *are reprinted in the* Musical News, *20 May 1899 (pp. 536–37) and in* L&PMTR, *15 June 1899 (p. 19).*

Other questions are discussed in the hearings and are reported in L&PMTR, *15 July 1899 (pp. 19, 21): French performing rights and* petits droits, *date of expiry of copyrights, and free trade in international copright.*

1 October 1899
'"Grove's Dictionary" has become a household word', but this does not mean every household has one. Novello & Co., however, are about to issue the four volumes plus Index (in cloth) for £2, less than half the original cost of £4 11s. 6d. Instalment buying is possible—six monthly payments of 7s. each.

Musical Times, p. 664

February 1900
The Music Publishers Section of the London Chamber of Commerce meets again on 16 January to confer with composers about the ramifications of the unfavourable 13 December decision of the Supreme Court of Appeal in the Boosey vs. Whight case, first tried in May, 1899.[125] Few composers attend, but expressions of support for some combined action are received from, among others, Parry, Mackenzie, Adams, Stanford, Elgar, and German. A letter will be sent to the House of Lords Special Committee containing the publishers' and composers' views on the unauthorized reproduction of pieces for mechanical instruments. *MO&MTR*, p. 357

March 1900
Patriotic pieces abound in new issues of publishers. Mr. Day, of Francis, Day & Hunter, tells the *MO&MTR* that they have been printing 'several ten thousand editions' of Stuart's *The Soldiers of the Queen*.[126]

The speed with which such works are rushed to print is illustrated by Mr. Broome's publication of *Imperial Volunteers March*. The plates were put in hand on Monday evening and by Thursday 5,000 copies were ready for distribution. Two weeks later a second edition of 10,000 copies was being prepared.

MO&MTR, pp. 428–29

15 April 1900
A special meeting called by the Music Publishers Sub-section of the London Chamber of Commerce considers Lord Monkswell's Bill which is now before the House of Lords. In its earlier meetings, a strong committee had drawn up a thorough report criticizing provisions of the Bill and offering suggestions for its improvement.

A four-page article prints these reports and discussions on some of the sections of the bill: 1) the 'mechanical instrument question'; 2) the 'right to copy music'; 3) 'first performance should be authorized performance'; 4) 'performing vs. publishing rights'; 5) monthly musical papers; 6) 'temporary copyright'; 7) 'divided colonial copyright'; and 8) something called 'sundry recommendations'. *L&PMTR*, pp. 11, 13, 15, 17

125. *Reported also in* L&PMTR, *15 Jan. 1900 (pp. 11,13). The actual hearing is summarized (p. 29) under 'Law Reports', and the decision not to appeal the case further to the House of Lords is reported in 15 Feb. 1900 (p. 11).*

The decision of the appeals court is deplored in a leading article in the Musical News, *23 Dec. 1899 (p. 561). See also* L&PMTR, *15 Jan. 1900.*

*Before this decision was reached, Whight had apparently disengaged, for it was reported at the 1 Nov. 1899 meeting of the MPA that he had 'parted company with his business' and had gone to America or Canada. Despite this, 'it was resolved to continue with the Aeolian in the Court of Appeals'. (*Min. Bk., *253).*

126. *A letter from the composer, Mr. Leslie Stuart, to the Attorney-General, pleading for his help in stamping out the pirates, was reprinted two years earlier in the* L&PMTR, *15 April 1898 (p. 21). Stuart estimated his loss to the pirates at that time as £250. He and his publisher, after employing detectives for four months at a cost of over £100, discovered the printer who had, by that time, sold some 100,000 illegal copies of the work to the hawkers.*

June 1900

Another meeting of the Select Committee and Mr. Clayton again testifies.[127] He objects that the new bill does not settle the point raised by the judge in Boosey vs. Whight, that the word 'copy' must be defined to include perforated rolls.[128] [Their Lordships later assent.] He complains about a provision of the bill that says copying a book by hand for personal use is not infringement and points out that most musical works can be copied easily and quickly. [Their Lordships agree that the provision should not stand.] Mr. Clayton states that if the performing rights to a work are not reserved by a notice on all copies of a work, that right should be irretrievably lost.

Another witness calls their Lordships' attention to the law in Germany which treats perforated rolls and sheets as 'copies'. He notes that in nine months, 3,071 copies (perforated rolls) of a mazurka, *La Czarine*, were sold, and the copyright owners were paid the royalties. *MO&MTR*, p. 644

127. *Also reported in* L&PMTR, *15 June 1900 (p. 15).*

128. *A lengthy report, including transcriptions of testimony,* ibid. *(p. 27).*

A letter by Mr. Clayton to *The Times* is reprinted. It decries the unfair practice of transferring copyrighted music onto perforated rolls. The statute of 1842, the prevailing copyright law, does not cover the problem; 'in 1842 automatic melody was a quantité negligeable'. He notes the German law and its protection of composer and publisher and also the distinction between mechanical instruments such as music boxes, where the law does not apply, and those like the Aeolian which are fed the music in re-notated form. He concludes that 'mechanical execution has a deadening effect on the musical sense, checks the progress of art, and should only be turned to' as a last resort. *MO&MTR*, p. 649

July 1900

The Select Committee continues consideration of the two copyright bills now before the House. Mr. Murray from the Music Publishers' Association suggests registration, at Stationers' Hall, under the control of the Board of Trade, which would carry with it a proper entry in the Customs throughout the Empire. He proposes a reduction of the present registration fee to half a crown per item.

He comments on the right of the universities of Cambridge, Oxford, and Dublin, and the Advocates' Library in Edinburgh to apply for a copy of any book within twelve months of its publication, the book to be delivered at its publisher's expense. He wants the time cut to three months so stock will not have to be held a year or more; he wants to change the law to affect only copyrighted works; and he wants to eliminate the requirement for publishers to deliver at their own expense. *MO&MTR*, p. 717

February 1901

At a meeting of the music publishers held at the Chamber of Commerce, 7 January, a letter is read inviting the British publishers to participate in sections dealing with the publication of music at the Fourth International Congress of Publishers scheduled for 9–12 June in Leipzig. Special topics will include 'discount in the music trade', and several members suggest adding a discussion of the reproduction of copyrighted works on the Aeolian.

The membership unanimously approves joining and participating in the Congress.[129] *MO&MTR*, p. 362B

129. *Fully reported also in* L&PMTR, *15 Feb. 1901 (pp. 7, 9).*

May 1901

George Augener (of the firm), in a 16 April letter to the editor of *The Times*, sounds alarmed at the possible inclusion of provisions of the Berne Convention in the new Copyright bill. He notes that large amounts of money spent by British publishers revising, fingering, translating, and engraving good works by foreign composers, then sold cheaply in England for many years, is a practice that would have to cease if clauses of the Berne Convention are ruled to apply retrospectively. Music works will cost far more.

A 21 April letter from Edwin Ashdown to *The Times* cites evidence and quotes phrases from the new bill to allay Mr. Augener's fears; there will be no retrospective application of Berne Convention strictures.[130] *MO&MTR*, p. 574

130. *Other responses to Mr. Augener's letter of 16 April (printed in full) and his own comments of 25 April on those responses appear in the* L&PMTR, *15 May 1901 (pp. 11, 13).*

June 1901

Two notices from the *Cork Constitution* describe the efforts of music retailers in cities such as Brighton, Glasgow, and now Birmingham to fight 'the music ring', as they call some leading music publishers.[131] It is pointed out that provincial musicsellers pay a shilling and four pence 'first hand' for a piece, plus carriage in many instances, the same price that the publishers charge the public. Moreover, the publisher will allow no return or credit on unsold stock. 'Combinations' of music retailers are agreeing not to sell for less than one and six; one writer wishes it raised to one and eight. *MO&MTR*, p. 649

131. *Though it does not mention 'music rings' or 'combinations', an article in* L&PMTR, *15 July 1900 (p. 13) comments favourably on similar actions taken by the Glasgow and other Associations and by the recently-formed Liverpool Music Trades Association.*

July 1901

A 'Disgusted' musicseller declares that the real difficulties in making a legitimate profit are (a) the forcing of novelties and (b) the refusal of the publisher to accept less than one-third for collecting orders. He claims dealers create popularity for a piece, not the publishers; when they must re-order it, they are forced by the publishers to pay full price. *MO&MTR*, p. 719

August 1901

Calling himself 'Eight-thirty', a writer applauds 'Disgusted's' letter and urges him to join a combination. 'Complaint', in another letter, agrees with 'Disgusted' and lodges additional protests about publishers. He notes that travellers visit teachers in his area and sell to them cheaper than he can—'nothing short of robbery'.[132] He proposes a nationwide union of dealers, headquartered in London (where the publishers headquarter) to regulate prices of music, look into unfair practices and complaints. Dealers would refuse to sell stock of publishers whose practices were deemed unfair or harmful to the trade.

A teacher, Mr. Tindall, exhorts the teachers to unite to publish, sell and exchange each other's works. He is obliged to sell pieces to his pupils at the price he pays the publisher; 'is this fair?' he asks. He complains about dealers being compelled to take the publishers' novelties and that the 'publishing ring' are not musicians at all. They do not know colleges, examinations, or letters after peoples' names, and counterpoint, canon, and fugue are as Greek to them.

MO&MTR, p. 790

132. *The* L&PMTR *reprints in 15 June 1901 a circular letter sent in April to music publishers by the Scottish Music Trades Association complaining about this practice and requesting that it be stopped. The circular is signed by eighty dealers. The editors of the* L&PMTR *comment on the problem in the 15 July 1901 issue, calling it 'an old one'. An original copy of the circular has not come to light. (See 'Missing Documents', Appendix, pp. 143–4).*

A report about the Fourth International Congress of Publishers in Leipzig in June indicates a considerable number of music publishers in attendance. Papers were read by Henry Clayton, Arthur Boosey, Oscar van Hase, David Day, and Henri Hinrichsen.[133] Day's, concerning piracies of copyright music by street hawkers is summarized [reprinted in its entirety in the September issue, pp. 867–68]:[134] Though the songs pirated are mostly music hall or popular songs with an ephemeral sale—popular but not for more than a few weeks—and though the publisher hopes to get only about a shilling a copy, it is very exasperating, nonetheless, to find illegal copies from some unknown printing press being sold by hawkers in the street for a penny or twopence.

Other subjects discussed were an international arrangement for marking a net price on music, and a law to prevent illegal reproduction of copyright music on mechanical instruments.

The editor, in a separate column notes that Lord Avebury ('who ought to mind his own business') has offered a bill that all music shops are to close at a certain time. Another 'fussy faddist' has offered a bill to spy on the poor who do work in their own houses. One section of this bill makes it 'an offence for a mother to suckle her babe after 7:45 in the evening!' *MO&MTR*, p. 795

133. *The reports were: 'Territorial Subdivision of Copyright Property', by Henry Clayton; 'Published Price and Discount in the Music Trade', by Henri Hinrichsen; 'Appropriation of Copyright Music by the Manufacturers of Mechanical Instruments such as the Aeolian', by Arthur Boosey; 'International Understanding of the Music Trade', by Oscar van Hase; and 'Piracies of Copyright Music', by David Day.*

134. *Reprinted also in the* L&PMTR, *15 Aug. 1901 (pp. 31–32) and in the* Era. *All of the papers are summarized and discussed* ibid., *15 July 1901 (p. 15) and in the* Musical Times, *1 July 1901 (p. 477). A two-page printed copy of Day's talk is also tipped into the* Min. Bk. *at page 266.*

September 1901

More replies to earlier letters are printed. Mr. Bishop of Holloway, N. blames the ruinous condition of the music trade on the wholesale houses, because they have continued to supply stores that sell below Bishop's retail prices.

Mr. Wilkes, a musicseller's assistant, noting that the publishers 'so far seem to have very few friends', calls Mr. Tindall's letter in the August issue bitter and unjust. He sees failure for an association of teachers and points out that only the publishers so reproved by Mr. Tindall can successfully market compositions.

MO&MTR, p. 870

October 1901

William Boosey of Chappell & Co. writes to remind readers that at his suggestion some years ago the London music publishers invited the retail music trade to meet with them and discuss the question of pricing.[135] The publishers urged the dealers to form an association (which they did) and then that they agree not to sell to the public below certain price schedules. If they would agree to that, the publishers would, in turn, 'supply journey orders to no retail music house outside their association'.

135. *But compare 15 Aug. 1896!*

The dealers balked because Army and Navy stores, as well as similar organizations, would not cooperate, according to the dealers. Mr. Boosey got a promise of such cooperation from the manager of the Army and Navy stores, still the dealers felt the association was impractical and nothing further came out of the scheme. *MO&MTR*, p. 63

'Territorial Subdivision of Copyright Property', a paper read by Henry Clayton (Novello, Ltd.) at the recent Leipzig congress, is reprinted in full. He contends: 'The Berne Convention removes all unnecessary formalities affecting the acquisition of copyright in country foreign to the country of origin . . . Yet the frequently international contracts which are being made between music publishers of different countries for the acquisition of copyright interests as between country and country' are creating difficulties and embarrassments. To solve the problems Clayton proposes: 1) that the original publisher, after dividing his copyright, print on all copies issued by him the name and address of each foreign publisher to whom portions of the copyright have been assigned, and 2) all purchasers of those copyright portions advertise the acquisition of copyright for each piece, with full particulars, in the 'official newspapers of their respective countries'. *MO&MTR*, p. 63

November 1901

In yet another letter decrying the practices of publishers, Mr. Joseph Bishop concludes, 'Pawnbrokers sell small goods, but they are too shrewd to dabble in sheet music'. *MO&MTR*, p. 142

Elsewhere it is noted that 'At Southport, society is at home again and the winter season has begun. Concerts and dances [and other musical, social functions] will occupy well to do residents for the next few months. This will be good for the music trade . . .'

MO&MTR, p. 142

December 1901

'Appropriation of Copyright Music by Mechanical Instrument Makers', Arthur Boosey's paper read at the Leipzig conference is reprinted. It points out that though music publishers have not thought it worthwhile to stop the reproduction of their copyrights for hand organs and musical boxes, they have not condoned it either, for such transfers invariably 'vulgarize' the tunes. More faithful reproduction of those copyright songs on an ordinary pianoforte by means of a perforated roll, however, constitutes a serious infringement of copyright. Unfortunately these instruments, such as the Aeolian, were practically unknown and were not considered when the Berne Convention was adopted, and in England, because such discs and rolls are not included in the definition of 'book' under English copyright law, they are presently immune.

The law is iniquitous; it prohibits the reproduction of a painting by means of photography without the owner's permission, but printed music can be reproduced by other means without any consideration for the owners. Rolls are being published containing songs in various keys which serve as accompaniment for singers who do not buy the printed music. Those giving dances can rent an Aeolian with all the latest rolls rather than hire a performer to play from printed music. In the future, these instruments are likely to become so perfected that 'music in the home by ordinary means may become almost superfluous . . . Parents will not press their children to persevere with their music lessons'.

He reviews the case of Boosey vs. Whight, disputes the judge's decision favouring Whight, and indicates future action on the problem. He disagrees with those who think that making it more difficult to appropriate songs for the Aeolian and other machines would interfere seriously with an important, growing trade. 'The interests of kindred trades should not be allowed to influence legislation when dealing with copyright as a property'.

MO&MTR, pp. 222–23

Some Music Trade Rhymes.

BY "OOT."

No. II.

SUGGESTED BY THE RECENT MANCHESTER CONFERENCE.

TUNE: "*The Better Land.*"

I've heard a tale of a far off town,
Where the lion and the lamb lie down;
Tell me where is that happy shore
Where the trade gets more than one and four.
Is it London great where the big wholesalers
Protect (?) the rights of the poor retailers?
Not there, not there, my boy!

Is it far away in some calm retreat,
Far, far from the din of Regent Street;
Where the cows stare into the dealer's store,
And inquisitive hens its recesses explore;
Where business is quiet and rents are low,
With a lamentable absence of "go?"
Not there, not there, my boy!

Edinburgh town is the place, my boy,
Where no rival traders each other annoy;
They list to requests with hearty approval
From each other for a tuner or a van for removal,
And if one's hard up with a bill to meet,—
But no, I've not heard they are *just* so sweet
In Auld Reekie's toon, my dear boy!

MO&MTR, p. 223

January 1902

The transcript of the paper read by Mr. Hinrichsen in Leipzig offers six principles which, the editor thinks, all English and foreign music publishers ought to endorse and enforce.

1. The published price fixed by the publisher is the basis for the sale of music and customary discounts. Though there are quarrels with the discount system, abolishing it is impossible. Any regulations dealing with pricing and discount need to be the common adoption of associations in various countries working through an international committee.

2. Musicsellers should try to reach an understanding in each country about the variation in fixed price related to the foreign rate of exchange. The international committee might be able to set a standard.

3. The custom of printing too high a price upon pieces of published music should be abolished. Excessive published prices increase the entire discount system.

4. Rules for sale to the public in each country should be drawn up by special associations and communicated to like associations in other countries with a request that the rules be observed. The international committee could enforce conformity.

5. 'An approximate uniformity in the highest discount allowed to the various countries (for net and ordinary articles) should be aimed at'.

6. 'Every open offer of discount to the public must cease'.

MO&MTR, pp. 304–06

Sheet Music Troubles.

BY "THE SHEET COLLECTOR."

I've heard it said, and I've seen for sure
That sheet music sellers are very poor;
But how, Oh how, do they usually grow
Pianoforte dealers with mighty show?
Can it be that publishers first give them a hand
By stocking their shops throughout the land?
Have care, can't say, my child!

I've heard their cry both near and far
Of the smallness of profits they say there are;
But can anyone tell me what they pay,
And when, Oh when, is their settling day.
Can it be that travellers book orders for cash
Which makes them appear so full of dash?
Have care, can't say, my child!

Now I've seen some publishers have their day,
But how rarely that happens I scarce need say;
Their risk is great, their expenses heavy
And copyright stock precarious, very.
A success in ten years, long credit in others,
My sympathy rests with our publishing brothers.
Right here, right there, my boy!

This song may be sung to any tune, providing that permission is first obtained from the publishers of the music selected.

MO&MTR, p. 306

February 1902

Some Music Trade Rhymes.

By "Oot."

No. 4.—THE MUSIC PUBLISHERS.

(After Kipling.)

To be taken "Cum grano salis."

Ye poured forth from the press without stint,
  Ye called on the wide world to see,
Ye delved in a mountain of rubbish
  To produce one good novelty.

And ye asked the composers inspired,
  And others whose silence were best,
To send in their wares, and were flooded
  With scores ye'd no knowledge to test.

For ye took up the good and the bad,
  And passed them all through your mill;
For ye said if we don't know what's what,
  The great stupid public soon will.

Ye laughed with a glee quite Satanic
  When ye booked from a poor purblind trade
The orders they gave ye, Titantic,
  Expecting their fortunes were made.

And then when their shelves were all loaded
  With stuff they could not realise,
Some made it straightway into parcels
  Of quite Brobdignagian size;

And showed in their windows a placard,
  Clear printed in letters immense,
Offering two or three pounds' worth of music
  For the small sum of twenty-four pence!

And then ye came round for your money,
  And made the poor dealer feel ill
When ye, with enduring persistence,
  Pressed for settlement of "little bill."

What! pay for the sheets that ye promised
  And vowed would be easy to sell;
Go, look at that card in the window,
  And note the sad tale it doth tell!

For when, as ye turn to your trinkets,
  And loll on your cushions so fine,
When smoking the choicest tobacco
  Or drinking your clear sparkling wine,—

Just think of the poor musicseller,
  If so you can do *sans* affright;
Just think of him there as he ever
  Looks sadly out into the night.

As his cry goes out to the darkness,
  And he knows not which way to turn;
He thinks of his old fire insurance,
  But the sorry stuff won't even burn!

So with a laugh soulless and mirthless,
  And words of a sulphurous hue,
He blows out the light,—for his last chance
  Has miserably now failed him too!

Out of the bitter comes sweet, and ere long
  His premises soon 'gin to grow;
For he's learnt that to live he must now
  To the pianoforte trade quickly go.

But think ye he does this to pile up
  A great store of silver and gold;
Think ye that he prospers a whit more
  Though his pianos and organs are sold?

Ah, no! though I think ye will doubt me,
  Believe it or not as ye will,—
The profits on pianos and organs
  Only settle the publisher's bill!

MO&MTR, p. 387

April 1902

Music Trade Rhymes.

By "Oot."

No. 5.—A Traveller's Reminiscence.

Tune: "The Children's Home."

I started my journey northward,
  My bag full of novelties
By Tosti, by Jude, and by Aylward,
  All garnished with royalties.
But there was one,—'twas a wonder,
  A better there never could be,
It's sale all the rest would outnumber,—
  A second "Jack's Yarn" or "Nance Lee."

Oh, when they had given me that song,
  I jumped with keen relish to see
'Twas a song that could not go far wrong,
  So I grasped at the work eagerly.
And by fifties and hundreds I sold it,
  My journey that time was a treat;
The number I booked, if I told it,
  You'd say would be quite hard to beat!

Ah, me! when I think of that journey,
  It seems all a beauteous dream;
For well know I that, ne'er again,
  Will such a song ever be seen.
But I just travel round with the others,
  Good and bad, whatever betide;
It's not long ere a trav'ller discovers
  That music shelves are conveniently wide.

MO&MTR, p. 544

In a column entitled 'Man in the Street', the writer, who calls himself 'A Spectator', deplores the cowardice of the pirates, derides the ineptness of lawmakers, despairs over the cost to publishers of enforcing their rights, and admits to having wondered what the Star Chamber or other tribunals might do to those taking the law into their own hands. With obvious glee he recounts the recent activities of the publisher Francis, Day & Hunter, which the *MO&MTR* reported as follows:

'Armed with a detective agency and trusty followers', Mr. Day, in January, seized 500 copies to test whether the 'pirates' could retaliate and how the law tribunals would respond. 'Emboldened by success they next attacked a cottage at Dalston and got 15,000 copies out of a van'. An attack on a barrow yielded 4,000 copies. A further haul of 8,000 was taken from a hawker's lodgings. Some chambers near the Mansion House produced 20,000. At a cottage where copies were being distributed through the window, one of the party dressed himself as a hawker and, passing muster, blocked the window. The aggrieved inmates summoned a policeman who declined to interfere, 'and a sort of siege of Badajoz in mild form took place. The sturdy assailants battered in the door with a cart tail, routed the defenders, and bore off 15,000 copies'.

MO&MTR, p. 552

The Music Trades Section of the Chamber of Commerce and the Music Publishers' Association meet together to consider an invitation from several organizations of book publishers[136] who wish them to join in urging, by petition and deputation, early legislation on the copyright question. Many speak strongly about the necessity of stopping the pirates, and it is unanimously resolved to assist the efforts of the book publishers. An 'authoritative statement of facts' in the piracy of copyright songs is to be drawn up and sent to the press by the Chamber of Commerce. *MO&MTR*, pp. 552–53

136. *The Publishers' Association of Great Britain and Ireland, the Society of Authors, and the Copyright Association, as reported in the* L&PMTR *for 15 April 1902 (pp. 19, 21) and recorded in the* Min. Bk., *276.*

Lord Monkswell's Copyright Bill [see July 1898] reprints and applies to musical copyright four clauses of the Copyright Bill of 1900 granting additional and summary powers to stop piracy of musical works. By Clause I a pirate (defined) could be liable to a penalty not exceeding five pounds for every illegal copy. Clause II[137] would permit a specially authorized constable to seize pirated copies without a warrant and bring them before summary jurisdiction. Clause II[138] would also allow the court of summary jurisdiction to grant warrants to search and seize pirated copies. Clause III provides that a constable, authorized by the apparent owner of a musical copyright, could seize pirated copies being 'hawked about'.

Piracy has reached alarming proportions, having a paralyzing effect on the legitimate trade. *MO&MTR*, p. 554

137. *Lord Monkswell's complete Memorandum accompanying this bill is reprinted in the* L&PMTR, *15 April 1902 (p. 25).*

138. *cf.* L&PMTR, *15 April 1902 (p. 21, col. 2).*

'Anti-Pirate's' letter notes that Sir Arthur Sullivan's estate and a host of other royalty owners are suffering terribly from the pirates' activities, and that the retail trade is about to be destroyed. Nevertheless, the Lord Chancellor and Mr. Balfour, judged by their recent remarks, wish 'to afford rogues every facility for continuing the frauds'.[139] He recommends the Association organize an army of

139. *This is the Right Honourable Gerald William Balfour, 2d Earl of Balfour, President of the Board of Trade from 1900 to 1905. See 'Dramatis Personae,' p. 3.*

500 young men split into 'commandoes' of twenty or so, raiding frequently the London and suburban market places, destroying pirated copies, 'and standing no nonsense'. *MO&MTR*, p. 554

A group comprised of the firms Boosey, Chappell, Hopwood & Crew, Francis, Day & Hunter, Sheard, Dean, Witmark, and John Church has announced the formation of a 'Copyright Association'[140] organized to take immediate steps for the prevention of piracy, a 'crying evil'. The Association plans to use every inducement to get [Lord Monkswell's] bill passed quickly. They urge others to join their efforts. *MO&MTR*, p. 555

140. *The Copyright Association was also discussed in an article in the* Daily News *which was reprinted in the* L&PMTR *for 15 April 1902 (p. 21), captioned, 'A Society for Self Defence'.*

J. George Morley, a musicseller, has received a circular from a group calling itself the Musical Copyright Association for the Suppression of Piracy.[141] It asks for money and moral support 'to eradicate the threatened annihilation of the music selling industry'. According to Morley, the music selling industry—having already been annihilated by the publishers—has hardly any fear of the piracies, and he doubts that any musicsellers will help in this matter which is exclusively the publishers' problem. He thinks they killed the music selling industry ten or twenty years ago by selling to individuals and professors at the same prices as those offered dealers. *MO&MTR*, p. 555

141. *No copy of the original circular has been found. See 'Missing Documents', Appendix, pp. 143–4).*

15 April 1902

Two applications have been made to the High Court for injunctions to keep the publishers' raiders from again trespassing on certain premises occupied by pirate publishers. The applications are dismissed. *L&PMTR*, p. 23

May 1902

Mr. Mullen, Secretary of the new Musical Copyright Association, points to progress in stamping out the sales of illegal reprints. The pirates are altering their methods, now reproducing popular and favourite operas, like Sidney Jones' *The Geisha*, and spreading their activities into the provinces. The Association is stepping up its efforts in those areas. It is also considering penalizing the public under the old Copyright Act of 1842 for buying piracies. 'Our agents are going around to the prominent hawkers and are taking the names . . . of persons thus illegally purchasing the copies with a view to making an example of them'. Prominent composers and musicsellers are joining the Association's efforts which have already yielded over a quarter of a million seized copies and a large number of printing blocks. The group wants 'to go quietly and kindly about the business', breaking no laws, but without proper legislation, 'our people may . . . get out of bounds'. The Association is not only dealing with the hawkers but is now going to the printers, 'asking them to surrender quietly'.[142]

MO&MTR, p. 627

142. *No documents relating to the activities of this group have come to light, other than reports in journals and newspapers. Many of the members were leaders of the MPA, but the MPA* Min. Bk. *does not include materials from this new organization.*

*Because the Copyright Association enjoyed considerable success against the pirates and with Parliament, however, at the MPA annual meeting a year later, on 16 June 1903, it was put to a vote to wind up the MPA. The resolution lost, 'consequently, the Association will continue, at all events, for the present'. (*Min, Bk., *285).*

An article from the *Yorkshire Post* offers several reasons for the great increase in piracies: the publishers' disinclination to produce cheap music, and their very sizeable profits, at 18d., for each piece. 'The Association has formed a sort of police . . . seizing and tearing up private stocks of hawkers and small shopkeepers'. Much money has been spent in High Court proceedings to restrain piracies of *Mona*, *The Holy City*, *Dolly Gray*, and other popular 'and often worthless songs'. Publishers desire that the sale of illegal reprints should be made a penal offence; despite their pronouncements, it is doubtful that their motivation is the interest of the composers—or of the public. The public's interest is, in fact, in cheap music, 'and the classical as cheap as any other'. The enormous sales of the pirates' products ought to convince the copyright proprietors that such editions would pay. *MO&MTR*, p. 628

'A Pirate's Ship Overhauled!' Boosey & Co. win a case against J. Poole & Sons, printers, in respect to the printing of some 5,000 copies of *The Holy City*.[143] The copies do not bear the name of the printer, a violation of the act of 1869. Though difficult, Boosey discovered that Poole had printed them for A. J. Bolton of Barge Yard, who 'had no means at all'. Bolton claimed to be acting only as an intermediary for someone named Jinks, address unknown. Boosey, therefore, could take action only against Poole & Sons.

143. *Also reported, with a partial transcript of the trial, in the* L&PMTR, *15 May 1902 (pp. 19, 21).*

George Boosey testifies that *The Holy City* has been very profitable, forty to fifty thousand copies having been sold at prices ranging from 2s. to 1s. 4d. Originally the composer and singer were to get royalties of 3½d. each per copy. The hawkers have been selling copies at 6d.—a higher price than usual for a pirated copy—because of the work's popularity. To date, 400 illegal copies have been seized.

His Lordship is bothered by the absence of the printer's names on the copies, but defendant explains that 'in the case of trade printers it was not the custom for the name to appear'. He has been deceived by Bolton who told him the copyright had run out; 'when a song had been sung once in the halls there was no copyright in it'. His firm had printed about fourteen songs for Bolton, the total number of copies amounting to about 200,000.

His Lordship considers this a deliberate evasion of the copyright act and for printing *The Holy City* fines Poole & Son a total of £230.
MO&MTR, pp. 633–34

Meanwhile, at Lambeth police court, the magistrate, Mr. Hopkins, has dismissed two prosecutions by hawkers who claim to have been assaulted.[144] The first claims that while selling music in the Brixton Road the defendant, a private detective, knocked him down, battered him, and upset his music board. He is unable to tell the magistrate from whom he bought the music, to which Mr. Hopkins replies, '. . . you will have to stand the racket'.

Two other private detectives are charged with assaulting another seller in Brixton Road. The seller claims he was held from behind while his music was seized, then thrown to the ground on his back. He is unable to give the names of the people from whom he bought the copies, and Mr. Hopkins states that he will, therefore, 'have to stand the racket'.[145]
MO&MTR, p. 634

144. *The* L&PMTR, *15 April 1902 (p. 25) reports that in one of two similar cases brought to the North London Police Court in March, the assault charges were upheld, the Association's agent fined.*

145. *These cases are also reported,* ibid., *15 May 1902 (p. 19).*

August 1902

At West Ham Police Court another assault case is tried in July before Mr. Gillespie. Complainant's solicitor states that the defendant, an ex-detective, was acting as an agent of the Musical Copyright Association. He notes the Association's circular which concludes that their representatives are instructed to seize all pirated songs held by hawkers and others, leaving it to them, 'to seek whatever redress the law may give them'. The solicitor says this intimates that they intend to break the law, and it is time this 'organised hooliganism' is stopped.

Complainant testifies that he opened his door, was confronted by the defendant and four or five others. Defendant said he represented the Association, 'and I have come to search your house for all pirated copies you may have'. Complainant asked for a search warrant; defendant said two of the detectives with him had it. The group then rushed into the house, one of them holding him down on the stairs by his throat while the others searched. He got free, procured a poker, but his wife and a lodger got between him and the men, one of whom then pointed something at him and said, 'If you come near me, down you go'.

Cross-examined he admitted having a quantity of pirated music in the house which he had bought at Aldgate. Mr. Gillespie stopped this line of questioning, for the case was one of assault.

The wife and lodger testify, and their stories support the complainant's. The defendant's testimony, and that of his cohorts, is not convincing and does nothing to excuse their actions or the charge of assault. During their testimony, however, the defendant's solicitor manages to state that 'no less than 30,000 copies had been seized during the preceding week', and 3,000 were found during the raid on the complainant's house.

The magistrate asserts that the Association arrogated to itself powers which did not even exist; they had no business making such a raid. The assault was committed; the defendant is fined £3.[146]

MO&MTR, pp. 856–57

146. *The case is also reported in great detail in the* L&PMTR, *15 Aug. 1902 (pp. 27, 29).*

September 1902

From the *Evening Standard*: 'At a time when pirated craft cruise about the main and other thoroughfares of the metropolis', the contemplation of the enormous successes of some musical compositions is of more than ordinary interest. The composers' remuneration and publishers' profit are often at odds.

Though 400,000 copies of Strauss' *Blue Danube* were sold in a single year in England and America alone, and it earned £100,000 for the publisher, the composer received but £40 for his work. Sousa fared better. He parted with his first success for £7, but is said to have been paid £10,000 for the *Stars and Stripes Forever. Cheer, Boys, Cheer* brought its creator, Henry Russell, exactly £1 plus a £10 gift, while thirty-nine presses were turning out copies of it by the thousands. For his *Woodman, Spare that Tree*, Mr. Russell received 8s. 2d. Rossini received £80 for his *Barber of Seville*, the same amount Verdi realized for his first opera, *Oberto. Les Cloches de Corneville* was written by Planquette while he was earning about 4 francs a night as a pianist in a third-rate music hall. The publisher who gave 30,000 francs for the publishing rights made £2 for each franc outlay. Audran made something like £20,000 for the tuneful melodies of his *La Mascotte*.

The article closes by noting the extraordinary prices paid at auctions (almost all of them by Puttick & Simpson) for the plates and copyrights of popular works: £2,240 for Mascheroni's *For all Eternity* in November 1898 (originally offered to a publisher for £10—and refused!); £1,212 for Watson's *Anchored* at a sale in 1894; £1,810 for Smallwood's *Fairy Barque* (for which he originally received five guineas); £988 for a song called *Tatters* in 1898; and £1,178 for *The Sailor's Dream* in the same year.

MO&MTR, pp. 929–30

The 'New Copyright Act', when it comes into force on 1 October next, contains at least two new features for the protection of publishers' properties. An aggrieved proprietor can hand a written request to any policeman who can then seize illegal copies *without warrant*, take them before a court of justice, and have them destroyed. No penalty other than the destruction of the copies is called for.

A new definition of 'musical copyright' will cover perforated rolls, sheets, or discs with the addition of the words 'in any notation or system', and 'otherwise graphically produced or reproduced'.[147]

MO&MTR, p. 931

The Editor remarks on the extraordinary number of pirated reprints now to be found in the streets and cities in the provinces, the public's apparent indifference to their illegality, but pleasure at their 2d. price. *MO&MTR*, p. 939

147. *The Musical (Summary Proceedings) Copyright Act of 1902 (2 Edw. VII., ch. 15) received the Royal Assent on 22 July and is summarized thoroughly in the* L&PMTR, *15 Aug. 1902 (p. 15). The Act is analyzed and its weaknesses considered in a subsequent article, 15 Sept. 1902 (p. 11) where it is termed 'A Loosely Drawn Measure'.*

Though several deputations from the MPA had pushed for passage of the bill, I find no mention of its eventual success in the MPA's Minute Book*!*

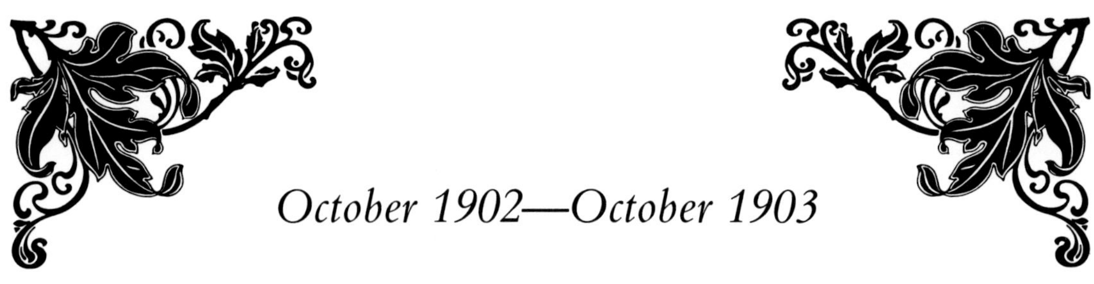

October 1902—October 1903

The war begins; publishers' agents mobilize; and the pirates raise their prices!

Tens of thousands of piracies are recovered in raids.

Moul sues Boosey for likening him to Wall.

Moul forms the British counterpart of the French Société.

Police courts begin to overflow with seized piracies; prosecutions are held up.

Anonymous hawkers frustrate the law.

The Commissioner of Police volunteers to store the piracies.

Sousa is shocked by the piracies, chided for his naiveté.

The hawkers advertise: 'all the best at 4d!'

Prosecutions under the Pedlars Act and the Vagrancy Acts are tried (but what is London?).

The Copyright Act of 1902 is 'of little use'.

The 'King of the Pirates' solemnly justifies his activities.

Musicsellers decide to organize to negotiate with the publishers.

A Musical Copyright Bill of 1903, with amendments, is presented.

Francis, Day & Hunter introduce 'Sixpenny Music'.

15 October 1902
On 1 October the war begins. The Metropolitan Police issue this 'Caution' to hawkers and pedlars [as reprinted in the *L&PMTR*]:

"The attention of hawkers, pedlars, and others is directed to the Musical (Summary Proceedings) Copyright Act, 1902 (2 Edward VII., chapter 15), which provides as follows :—

"'If any person shall hawk, carry about, sell, or offer for sale any pirated copy of any musical work, every such pirated copy may be seized by any constable without warrant, on the request in writing of the apparent owner of the copyright in such work, or of his agent thereto authorized in writing, and at the risk of such owner.

"'On seizure of any such copies, they shall be conveyed by such constable before a Court of Summary Jurisdiction, and, on proof that they are infringements of copyright, shall be forfeited or destroyed, or otherwise dealt with as the Court may think fit.

"'"Musical work" means any combination of melody and harmony, or either of them, printed, reduced to writing, or otherwise graphically produced or reproduced.

"'"Pirated musical work" means any musical work written, printed, or otherwise reproduced, without the consent lawfully given by the owner of the copyright in such musical work.'

"Instructions have been given to the constables of the Metropolitan Police to enforce the provisions of the above-mentioned Act, which comes into operation on the 1st day of October, 1902.

"A. C. Bruce,
"The Acting Commissioner of Police of the Metropolis."

Mr. Day, of Francis, Day & Hunter, President of the Music Publishers' Association, tells an interviewer from the *Westminster* that the new Bill provides for no right of search and no adequate penalties for infringement. 'We intend, however, to redouble our efforts . . . establishing agents all over the country with written authority from the firms interested . . . We have fifty ex-policemen . . . and any number of voluntary helpers. When we close business at four to-day we shall have from 800 to 1,000 in London alone searching for the enemy . . . We are watching the most notorious offenders—we have a list of two hundred or so . . .'

[This 'Authority' (as reproduced in the *L&PMTR*) was printed by the publishers and hundreds were broadcast to agents and music-sellers throughout the country.]

To
of
In pursuance of The Musical (Summary Proceedings) Copyright Act, 1902, Section 2, We, the undersigned,
Music Publishers, being the apparent owners of each of the under-mentioned Musical Works, and of the Copyright therein namely : —
[here follows the list of works]
do hereby as from the 1st day of October, 1902, appoint you our Agent and do hereby authorize you to, at our own risk, request in writing on enclosed blue forms, any Constable to, without Warrant, seize from any person or persons all pirated copies of the said Works or either of them which may be hawked, carried about, sold, or offered for sale by such person or persons.

Signed.............................

[The 'Authority' was accompanied by a 'Notice' to constables.]

To
Constable No.
In pursuance of The Musical (Summary Proceedings) Copyright Act, 1902, Section 2, I
of
in the (County, City, or Borough) of
being the Agent thereto authorized in writing by the apparent owners of the under-mentioned Musical Works and of the Copyright therein, namely :—

Alice, where art Thou ?
Because I love You
Better Land, The
Bird in the Gilded Cage, The
Brooklyn Cake Walk
By the Fountain
Crossing the Bar
Daddy
Down South Barn Dance
Dream of Paradise, A
Good-bye, Mignonette
Heavenly Song, A
Holy City, The
Honeysuckle and the Bee
I may be Crazy
Juliana
Killarney
Lost Chord, The
Ma Rainbow Coon
Maud, Maud, Maud (Toreador).
Mona
O Dry those Tears
Oh Flo (the Motor Car Song)
Ora Pro Nobis
El Capitan March (P. Sousa)
Everybody's loved by someone
Flight of Ages, The
For all Eternity
Frangesa March
Garden of Sleep, The
Gates of the West
Gift, The
Good-bye, Dolly Gray
Pliny, Come kiss yo' Baby !
Promise of Life, The
Queen of the Earth
Shade of the Palm, The
Six little Wives (San Toy)
Skylark, Skylark
Smoke, Smoke, Smoke
Star of Bethlehem, The
Star of my Soul
Stars and Stripes for ever March
Sunflower and the Sun
Tell Me, Pretty Maiden
Whisper and I shall Hear

request you to, without warrant, seize from the person whom I now show you the pirated copies of any of the said Musical Works he is now hawking or carrying about.

Signed..... ....

The article continues with a report that 'The street hawkers openly announced on placards September 30th as the last day, and their prices rose a good deal'. On the first day, 1 October, the

Association sent out over 1,000 men to hunt for pirates. 'All the publishers and musicsellers closed their premises at four o'clock and sent their employees into the street all over London to aid the army of detectives already at work'. *L&PMTR*, pp. 19, 21, 23

November 1902

An Occupation Gone.

Weep! for they take my goods away;
'Tis sad and strange as if to-day
The partridge on the hawk should prey,
To see musicians rob the hawker.
So, pillaged, plundered, sacked, I walk
The streets,—nay, cease from vulgar talk,
Don't, don't say "Walker!"

The public trust in me was placed,
And so with high and cultured taste
In music one and all were graced,
But now, oh! how the news must grieve you.
My trade is gone, and I must say
In truth "Good-bye, my Dolly Gray,
For I must leave you."

Cheap was sweet "Down the Vale" I know,
And cheap that moving strain "Oh, Flo!"
At twopence each I let them go,
For mine was never once a high rate.
But woe for us! its woe, I vow,
I, erst your benefactor, now
Am dubbed a pirate.

In vain to buy the public longs
For nothing but the high class songs,
And as they curse their growing wrongs,
Mine, in these Autumn days, grow riper.
For I, to live, must peddle toys,
Or, like those cultureless street boys,
Shout "Ev'nin' piper!" M. S.

MO&MTR, p. 152

148. *'Gone' is far too optimistic, for though the new Act has frightened some pirates, they have not been banished. Three requirements of the Act, along with serious omissions, make it difficult to effect, as the actions in various cases that are reported in the* L&PMTR, *15 Oct. 1902 (pp. 15, 21–23) and 15 Nov. 1902 (pp. 19, 21–23) point out: 1) the constable must be requested 'in writing' to seize suspected piracies; 2) a Certificate of Registration at Stationers' Hall must be produced for the magistrate, at some cost; 3) the hawker accused must be summoned, and he is usually a man without permanent address.*

December 1902

An article entitled 'Boarding "The Sugar Loaf" in Search of Pirates!' recounts another court case involving representatives of the Musical Copyright Association charged with breaking and entering. Mr. Cowl, solicitor for the complainant (and solicitor for the complainant in a similar case in August 1902 [q.v.]) admits that his client had a considerable quantity of pirated music (later put at 20,000 copies, 'two cab loads') stored in his room at 'The Sugar Loaf' beerhouse in Whitechapel. The complaint is that while his client was out, the defendants broke the lock on the door, entered without a warrant, and carted those copies away.

Defendants' solicitor admits all the charges are valid but insists the actions were justified by the severity of the 'piracy problem'.

The magistrate, Mr. Mead, though sympathetic to the publishers' problems, states that no person has a right to take the law into his own hands and decides for the complainant.[149]

149. *Also reported in detail in the* L&PMTR, *15 Nov. 1902 (p. 23).*

MO&MTR, pp. 228–29

Police-Sergeant Church and Mr. William Elliott (of Messrs. Gould & Co.) bring to the magistrate of Wolverhampton Police Court a bundle of pirated copies and ask that they be destroyed, under provisions of the new Musical Copyright Act of 1902 passed in October [but not reported in the *MO&MTR*!]. Mr. Elliott had 'made out an authority', and with Officer Church acting under his instructions, seized the music in the Market Hall the previous afternoon. The hawker seemed unperturbed, saying, 'I don't care, I've made my list. It cost me a farthing apiece and I made twopence. You won't get hold of the printer. I know him. But I won't part.'

The magistrate asks if the hawker is present and is told that he was invited to appear but refused. The music is ordered destroyed. Later, Mr. Elliott in an interview with a newspaper representative warns markets committees against renting stalls to hawkers selling illegal copies. 'Our agents will always be on the spot.'

MO&MTR, p. 238

January 1903

An interesting libel case is reported. Mr. Afred Moul, composer, managing director of the Alhambra Theatre and British representative of the Société des Auteurs, Compositeurs et Éditeurs de Musique, has sued Mr. William Boosey, managing director of Chappell & Co.

Responding to a letter from Moul in the *Daily Mail* of 12 March 1902, Boosey wrote the *Mail* to say that the copyright legislation, about which Moul had complained, is the short act of 1882 which was passed as a matter of urgency to assist the publishers in their dealings with 'a gentleman who was in Mr. Moul's own line of business'. The 'gentleman' to whom Boosey referred was Harry Wall, notorious for his oppressive actions against those performing copyrighted songs without permission, who was later imprisoned for pretending to be a solicitor.[150]

150. *More about Harry Wall's 'line of business' is in note 7 at November 1881. See also the Index.*

At the trial on Moul's complaint, Moul claims to have conducted his business honourably as representative of the French society; he has not conducted business by methods like Wall's and is damaged by Boosey's insinuation. Several witnesses give evidence about the reputation of Harry Wall.

Boosey says that when he wrote the letter he did not know of Wall's conviction, only that Moul and Wall each collected fees 'in respect of minor compositions'. However legitimate, the business inflicts hardships, because Moul could not publish a list of the songs owned by the society and only by joining the society could people avoid the risk of being sued. Boosey states that he is not hostile to the plaintiff, though opposed to the society he represents.

Verdict is for Moul, the plaintiff, for £150 damages.[151]

MO&MTR, p. 312

151. *An extensive report of other litigation between the Société and Chappell & Co is in the* L&PMTR *for 15 April 1900 (pp. 13, 15) and includes a valuable history of the Société and full description of the workings of the* petits droits. *A transcript of further hearings on the case appears in the same journal for 15 June 1900 (p. 30).*

February 1903

An article reprinted from the *Morning Advertiser* calls attention to the poor treatment and miserly recompense afforded composers by prevailing copy- and performing-rights statutes. Legislators are not artists and are not very understanding of their problems. Questions appealing to the 'commercial mind' are understood and improvements follow. If a poacher shoots a partridge he goes to gaol, but musical pirates flaunt the existing laws and, at worst, pay only a small court cost. The legislators take a personal interest in game laws.

Publishers have no interest in performing rights, the article says, viewing them as impediments to business. Vocalists are paid to sing certain works for whose performance the creator receives only what may arise from the sale of other copies.

MO&MTR, pp. 291–92

Mr. Moul, Director of the Alhambra Theatre and for many years the English representative of the Société des Auteurs, Compositeurs et Éditeurs de Musique, is about to devote full time to forming an English branch of that organization. He has pointed out that the society's revenues from performance fees for the past year amounted to £100,000. 'Not a single piece of music by a French composer is allowed to be performed [in Britain] without paying toll' to the composer through the Société.

MO&MTR, p. 392

Difficulties with the new Musical Copyright Act have forced its suspension in all the Metropolitan Police Courts waiting the outcome of an appeal by Francis, Day & Hunter of a previous decision by the Marylebone police magistrate. The proceedings of the appeal are reprinted in the *MO&MTR* along with a commentary on the case from the *Standard.* The point at issue is complicated but crucial to the functioning of the new Act:

A constable seized a quantity of pirated songs, brought them to the Marylebone court of summary jurisdiction, along with the verified owner, Francis, Day & Hunter, who asked that the magistrate order the copies destroyed or handed over to the owners. The magistrate refused because the hawker had not been issued a summons to appear in court in accordance with the summary jurisdiction acts, but was merely advised by the constable of the time and place of the hearing.

Appellant's solicitor points out several problems. Under the new act there is no machinery to ascertain the names and addresses of the hawkers and no machinery providing for the manner in which seized copies are to be dealt with. (In its commentary, the *Standard* points out other deficiencies: Likening pirated copies to unfit meat, they say the constable should have power to destroy without previous issue of a summons, i.e., the power of detention until inquiries have been made. Penalties—fines—are needed for those guilty of hawking pirated copies. Summary searches of the premises of anonymous publishers and printers must be permitted, and courts must be able to deal with them in like manner as their 'impecunious and wastrel' agents.) Because there is no clear direction about what is to be done with seized copies, the police commissioner, asserting that police offices and courts cannot be made warehouses, will not take those copies in until summonses have been served on the hawkers. As solicitor for the appellant observes, without other machinery to detain the hawker, the whole act can be defeated simply by the hawker refusing to answer an 'invitation' to appear or to give his true name and address.

The magistrate, with 'the other learned judges concurring', dismisses the appeal, however, because he feels the courts should not 'depart from a well known principle of criminal law'; magistrates do not have *ex parte* powers under the acts as passed.[152]

MO&MTR, pp. 395–96

152. *Fully reported as well in the* L&PMTR *for 15 Feb. 1903 (p. 19), which calls it a 'Deadlock.'*

In a letter to the *MO&MTR*, the Lancashire Traders' Association reminds readers that unpaid income tax for 1902–03 is now called for, that many businesses and manufacturers overlook certain deductions for machinery repairs and replacement, for life insurance, and other expenditures. They offer to advise readers, 'gratuitously', about their claims if they will write the Association.

MO&MTR, p. 397

Henry Glibbery of West Norwood, after reading the decision of the Appeal Court, now wonders 'whether a further act of parliament will be asked for by the music publishing houses to help them in demanding the absurdly high prices now charged for copyright songs!' One shilling and fourpence for a single song is a luxury only for millionaires; that market is dead. No one now should expect to make £17,000 for an afternoon's work on a single song, as was the case with *The Lost Chord.* The legislature cannot be expected 'to pass acts session after session to perpetuate . . . an unwarranted extortion'.
MO&MTR, p. 397

'A Way Out of a Difficulty', seems to have appeared. The Lord Mayor, with nineteen piracy cases before him, hears from Mr. Rutland, the representative of the Music Copyright Association, that in the first case the hawker has refused to tell his name and address. Under the recent court decision, then, all he can do is ask that the copies seized remain in the hands of the police. He cannot ask for a summons, for the hawker refused his name. At this point, a city inspector announces to the court that the Commissioner of Police will give free storage to seized parcels for twelve months, after which, if not dispersed, they will be destroyed.

The Lord Mayor reviews the provisions of the Copyright Act, sees no reason for the previous court decision insisting on summonses or for the lower court's decision to have been upheld on appeal. 'It appears to me absurd'. He is pleased by the Commissioner's decision and remarks that hawkers will know now that any property seized from them will be irretrievably lost. 'I am glad to find that the law is sometimes in accordance with common sense'.
MO&MTR, p. 400

The 'Man in the Street', whose earlier letter was printed in the April 1902 issue, writes again, though he is 'naturally a bit wearied of seeing paragraphs headed "Music Piracy"'. When he spoke before somewhat contemptuously of English law, he says, he 'little thought how strongly my comments would be justified by future developments . . . by this wretched act'. He contrasts legal language with 'Sane English', and supposes that another act will be needed to remedy matters.
MO&MTR, p. 401

A letter from John Philip Sousa to *The Times* is printed: 'We have a tradition in America that English law is a model to be emulated by all peoples. You can imagine my astonishment therefore, on arriving in London, to find that pirated editions of my compositions were being sold broadcast in your city!'[153]

153. *Half-a-dozen Sousa piracies available from hawkers for 2d. each were included by the pirates in a list they distributed in Shepherd's Bush. The list is reproduced below, 15 Feb. 1903.*

In a letter in response, Chappell & Co. sympathize with Sousa and take the opportunity to outline the provisions of legislation that would deal with the problem. *MO&MTR*, p. 398

15 February 1903

Sousa's surprise [see above] and ingenuousness are mildly chided, and he is given step-by-step instructions about how to thwart the illegal sale of, and to have destroyed, all piracies of his *El Capitan*.
L&PMTR, p. 21

'It is computed on the 7th inst., three-quarters of a million copies of pirated music had been seized'. This will afford some idea of the extent of this illicit traffic:

LIST OF PIRATED WORKS.

The following is a list of piracies left by the hawkers at houses in the Shepherd's Bush district, and to be called for : –

SIR OR MADAM,

Having purchased an enormous quantity of high-class music, we are able to supply the following pieces at ridiculously low prices (at 4*d.*) :

Asthore. H. Trotere.
Anchored. Michael Watson.
By the Fountain. Stephen Adams.
Brooklyn Cake Walk. T. W. Shurban.
Calvary.
Children's Home. F. H. Cowen.
Chorister. Sir Arthur Sullivan.
Dear Heart.
Deathless Army.
Dream of Paradise. Hamilton Gray.
Daddy. A. H. Behrend.
Dear Home Land. William Slaughter.
Double Eagle March.
Down South. W. H. Myddleton.
Down the Vale. Frank L. Moir.
Eileen Alannah.
Flight of Ages. Frederick Bevan.
For all Eternity. Angelo Mascheroni.
Gates of the West. Caroline Lowthian.
Garden of Sleep. Isidore de Lara.
Go 'way you Massa Bee.
Hill's March.
I Dreamed a Dream.
In Old Madrid. H. Trotere.
In Friendship's Name (As Friends We Met)
La Frangesa March. P. M. Costa
Motherland ('San Toy')
Maud, Maud. Gaiety Version
Nazareth. Chas. Gounod.
Ora Pro Nobis. M. Piccolomini.
Pliny, Come Kiss Yo' Baby. Dave Reed, jun.
Promise of Life. F. H. Cowen.
Sail Away (Tom Costello).
Star of Bethlehem. Stephen Adams.
Shade of the Palm. Leslie Stuart.
Skylark, Skylark. E. W. Rogers.
Some Day.
Star of my Soul. Sidney Jones.
Tact.
Tell Me Pretty Maiden (Duet). Leslie Stuart.
The Holy City. Stephen Adams.
The Gift. A. H. Behrend.
The Lost Chord. Sir Arthur Sullivan.
The Miller's Daughter ('Three Little Maids').
The Toilers. M. Piccolomini.
The Better Land. F. H. Cowen.
True till Death. Alfred Scott Gatty.

At 2*d.* : A Bird in a Gilded Cage; Alice, where art Thou; Because I Love You; Come Back, Asthore; Come Back to Erin; Dolly Gray; Everybody's Loved by Someone; El Capitan March; Father, Mother, and the Apple; Good-bye, Mignonette; Hail Spirit of Liberty (Sousa); Honeysuckle and the Bee; Honeymoon (March); I may be Crazy; I want to see the dear old home again; King Cotton March (Sousa); Killarney; Liza Johnson; Let go Eliza; Looping the Loop with Lucy; Maisey, my Maisey; Ma Rainbow Coon; Mary; Mona; My Daddy's a Gentleman; My Heart is Your Heart; O, Dry those Tears; Oh, Flo (Motor Car Song); Queen of the Earth; Santa Claus; Song of the Thrush; Stars and Stripes for Ever; Shepherd of Souls; The Blind Boy; The Boers have got my Daddy; The Horse the Missus Dries the Clothes on; The Invincible Eagle (Sousa); The Sunflower and the Sun; The Miner's Dream of Home; Three Women to Every Man; Whisper and I Shall Hear; Whistling Rufus; You can get a Sweetheart any day, but not another Mother.

Pianoforte selections, 12 pages (at 6*d.*) : Geisha; Floradora; Belle of New York; The Country Girl; San Toy; Toreador; Chinese Honeymoon, and a large variety of others.

L&PMTR, p. 23

154. *The list is one of the few things the pirates ever printed which belonged to them.*

A Mr. Wiltshire thinks music, despite what the publishers say, could be published cheaper. The engraving of music plates is not as expensive as they maintain, 'while the cost of transferring to lithographic stones, paper, and printing is now as cheap as letterpress printing'. *L&PMTR*, p. 25

Stephen Adams (Maybrick), Mayor of Ryde, Isle of Wight, writes, 'I have before me at the present moment no less than *seven* pirated editions of my song, 'The Holy City', and when I take walks abroad I have these pirated editions of my own works thrust in my face and am powerless to act . . .'. *ibid.*

From Brighton, a correspondent writes to say that the pirates 'are going strong', and that they have said they intend 'to clear out the regular music publishers' and start a shop of their own. *ibid.*

March 1903

Two 'unsuspected', subtle forms of copyright infringement are reported by a letter writer who has received stern responses from publishers to what he thought were innocent inquiries. The first reproof arose from his asking a publisher to issue his manuscript arrangement of 'an obbligato harmonium part as an addition to some extracts (arranged for violin and piano) from Gounod's two oratorios'. The letter—so threatening that he quotes from it—censures him for making 'manuscript corrections' to one edition of a classic from a later edition, though both were from the same publisher—the one doing the threatening—and he had paid for both copies!

The writer views the objections as unenforceable; they also invite 'ingenious endeavors to evade . . . the too small meshes of the doctrine'. *MO&MTR*, pp. 473–74

Reprinted from the *Daily Telegraph*: The Musical Copyright Act passed hurriedly during the late session of Parliament, coming into force last October, has not stamped out the evils of piracy. By the interpretations of several magistrates, upheld by the Lord Chief Justice and others of the High Court, the meaning of the Act seems to be contrary to the intention of those who made it. Piracy is so profitable that its agents draw up catalogues and send them broadcast, even to the sorry writers whose pockets they are picking. Constables are seizing these illegal sheets, but they cannot be destroyed because hawkers cannot be brought into court. 'There are no less than half a million copies of pirated songs stored away in Scotland Yard'. The law seems designed to protect the thief.

MO&MTR, p. 479

In police court a hawker is charged under a statute of George IV that he, 'being a petty chapman or pedlar, did wander abroad and trade' in certain illegal copies of music, without licence.

Mr. Rutland is again solicitor for the Musical Copyright Association, and a Mr. Cowl appears for the defendant. The magistrate, Mr. Curtis Bennett, recommends to proceed under the Pedlars Act[155] where a pedlar is defined as a man who travelled from town to town. Mr. Rutland, fearing that if this were the case the hawkers would simply confine their operations to one municipality, prefers to proceed under the Vagrant Act[156] where the offence was 'to wander abroad and trade', as had the defendant, hawking as a pedlar, without a licence.

The hearing adjourned with Mr. Cowl being told by the magistrate to be prepared to argue the point whether London was not a collection of towns.

ibid.

155. *Pedlars Act, 1871, 34 & 35 Vict., ch. 96, sec. 1–21, sched. 1, 2 and 1881, 44 & 45 Vict., ch. 45.*

156. *Vagrancy Act, 1884, 47 & 48 Vict., ch. 43 and 1891, 54 & 55 Vict., ch. 69.*

Summonses against various hawkers were heard in the same court. In several instances the summonses were served by identification (the hawkers' names and addresses being unknown, and in other cases, at false addresses). Mr. Curtis Bennett held in two cases that the service was good. He ordered the music destroyed but could levy only costs against each defendant because fines were not provided for in the new copyright act. In the future, he announced, he will increase the costs, payments to be enforced by distress, imprisonment in default of distress. All but one of the defendants were unable to pay and were committed for fourteen days. *ibid.*

Also at Marylebone, based on Magistrate Bennett's previous decisions, two hawkers were brought in charged as pedlars without licence. They were then served with summonses to show why the music should not be destroyed. They could not and were ordered to pay costs which they claimed they could not do. Mr. Curtis Bennett pronounced judgment: 'In default you must go to prison at once for twenty-one days. After this week I shall add hard labour to the imprisonment'.

ibid.

Mr. Coote, Managing Director of Hopwood & Crew publishers, points out the falling value of shares in music publishing firms, all because of the pirates. His firm's, within a few weeks, have dropped from £1 by $\frac{1}{4}$ to $\frac{3}{8}$ a share. He estimates the injury to the trade at millions of copies. 'Our trade customers cannot order from us; they say all the business is now done in the streets. The legitimate trade is completely paralyzed'.[157] *MO&MTR*, pp. 479–80

157. *The letter is also printed in the* L&PMTR *of 15 Feb. 1903 (p. 23).*

The provisions of a new copyright bill drafted by the Music Copyright Association are reviewed. The present act (October 1902) has been of little use, and though some success has been achieved in the war against the pirates by using the Vagrant Act of George IV and the Pedlars Act these do not reach the producer of illegal copies.

The new bill's provisions require that 1) the printer's name be placed on all music; 2) street pedlars be licensed (though this may cause some difficulties with matchsellers, newspaper boys, etc.); and 3) all penalties [i.e., fines] be summarily recoverable and, in default, imprisonment imposed. A search clause would give power to enter premises on reasonable suspicion. Lastly, there would be a penalty on every copy, because now a very large part of the illegal trade is done by post. *MO&MTR*, p. 484

The London correspondent of the *Glasgow Herald* has received information regarding piracy from the 'King of the Pirates' with headquarters in London—information which the 'King' presented before a departmental committee on musical copyright. The major points of his presentation are the pirates' definition of copyright ('Nonsense' snorts the *MO&MTR* in a footnote!), the need for cheap music for the masses, the unseemly profits of the publishers, and their failure to protect fully the interests of the composers. The pirates, according to the 'King', are quite willing to respect the full rights of the composers, but the publishers shelter themselves behind the composers, making it impossible to separate the two interests and to strike at the publisher in any other way. The publishers, especially those of the MPA, are a 'ring' whose sole purpose is to keep prices high.

A heated response to 'the lucubrations' of the 'pirate bold' is printed. Its author, the Assistant Secretary of the MPA, refutes, point by point, the pirates' argument, adding that 'copyright music is not a necessity, it is a luxury'.[158] *MO&MTR*, pp. 477–78

158. *Within a few months, by August 1903, all was not well with the Musical Copyright Association, judged by the minutes of a meeting of the Music Publishers' Association on 6 August 1903. It is reported that Chappell & Co. and Boosey & Co. have both withdrawn from the Musical Copyright Association, because its representative, a Mr. Willeby, wishes to deal with Parliament himself. Mr. David Day, Chairman of the MCA, was present at the meeting. He recapitulated 'the good work done by the MCA', noting 'the lifeless state of the MPA'. A resolution proposed by him, to give money to the MCA, was soundly defeated. The Secretary was instructed to write to Mr. Day [!] suggesting a joint meeting of the two memberships.*

This does not seem to have occurred. The minutes for a meeting of the MPA Committee on 23 Sept. 1903 state that William Boosey urged the MPA to 'embark on a more active policy with regard to the suppression of street piracies . . . no reason why the two Associations should not work together side by side'. (Min. Bk., *287–89).*

May 1903

The aesthetic shortcomings of pirated copies are touched on in an interview between the *Daily News* and a publisher's representative. 'The illicit copy of, say, *The Holy City* betrays a common and vulgar style of printing . . . When placed on a pianoforte in any respectable drawing room or music room it would be shabbily out of place ... They are produced in facsimile by a photographic process ... principally in Liverpool ... then sold in the provinces chiefly house-to-house. They do not pirate the failures' (which, he emphasizes, is why publishers' prices must remain high). There are eighteen printed editions of *The Holy City*, some mere blotches. Pirates, it is claimed, can print cheaply 500,000 copies, and stand to lose little even if some are confiscated. *MO&MTR*, p. 634

Finally beginning to organize, the Musicsellers' Association meets for the first time in Leeds in March, with its principal objects announced as: 1) to unite the *bona fide* musicsellers in the country; 2) to regulate the prices and prevent underselling; 3) to induce publishers to cease supplying the profession direct; and 4) to act in combination on any other matters affecting the interests of members.

Point three is of most immediate concern and is discussed at length. A mutual three-party arrangement—publisher, dealer, teachers—seems to be the only solution but difficult to effect.

MO&MTR, p. 635

June 1903

Lord Lytton has introduced in the Upper House amendments to the Copyright Act intended to correct all the defects and omissions that its implementation since October last has revealed. The bill of amendment, though it does take care of the difficulties, 'is twice the length of the old one, and there will therefore be two acts to construe instead of one ... Why such terribly involved English should be used ... passes the wit of man to discover'. The bill, called the Musical Copyright Act, 1903, includes these provisions: 1) It defines piracy and calls for fines of 5s per copy dealt with, as well as destruction of the stock. 2) It eliminates the need for proof that a summons has been served before the court can order destruction of the illegal copies. 3) It mandates that the publisher's true name and address appear on each copy. 4) The definition of 'pedlar' in the Pedlars Act of 1871[159] is now broadened to include hawkers of music in public places. *MO&MTR*, p. 716

159. *34 & 35 Vict., ch. 96, sec. 1–21.*

September 1903

'Mercury', in 'Trade Topics', states that the increased demand for everything pertaining to the performance of music has brought about increasing competition in the supply of the material. 'The good folk concerned have set themselves out to cater for the many instead of the few'. The workings of supply and demand make the provision of cheap music and musical instruments inevitable. Publishers of high class vocal and instrumental music must seriously consider the 'immensely larger sale which cheaper music would command . . . The plague of "pirates" has proved that those who produce popular music have not yet managed to reach the masses . . .' Pirates have succeeded only because they have 'happened to meet a public want'.

MO&MTR, pp. 947–48

October 1903

Under the caption, 'Sixpenny Music!' the *MO&MTR* discusses a 'Coming Revolution in the Music Publishing Trade'. Messrs. Francis, Day & Hunter have announced in the 24 September London *Daily Mail* their decision to publish sixpenny copies of popular songs to meet a popular demand, in the same way as the book trade has issued popular editions of well known novels. The first editions will be issued as usual at the price of 2s.; if they win wide popularity, then a sixpenny edition will follow.

The new departure is practically a result of the pirates and of 'an enormous new market for cheap music created by the rapid multiplication of pianos in working class homes'. In a few months, for example, the pirates sold a million copies of *Soldiers of the Queen*, while its rightful owner and publisher, in the same period, sold an additional 100,000. The song's author sees the sixpenny editions 'as an admission of the claims made by the defenders of the pirates that publishers have been robbing the public'.

Messrs. Chappell & Co. in a letter to the *Daily Mail* state 'there is not the slightest chance of the leading music publishers ever falling into line' with Francis, Day & Hunter's scheme. *MO&MTR*, p. 69

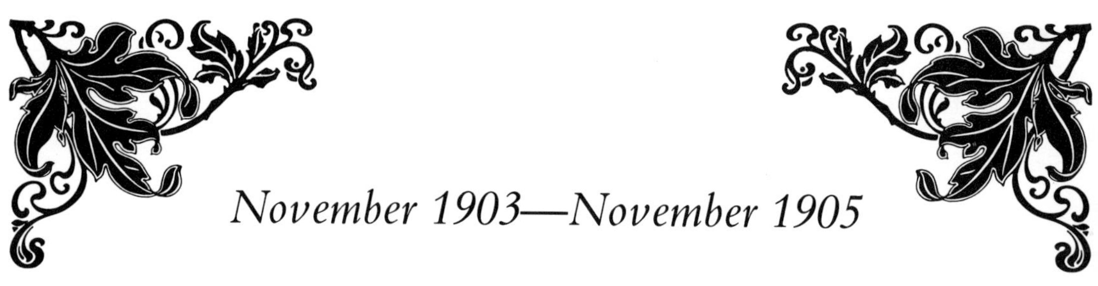

November 1903—November 1905

Arthur Preston, sleuth and prosecutor, enters the picture.

Dealers continue to voice discontent with publishers' practices.

To combat piracy, some say, publishers should lower their prices.

A printer in court admits to turning out 5,000 piracies a day.

The pirates' taste is scrutinized.

Mr. James Caldwell, M. P., begins his long fight against a good copyright bill, raising Mr. Boosey's ire.

Boosey, in a huff, responds to Caldwell's 'Manifesto'.

A 'Great Protest Meeting' takes place.

The publishers announce they will cease buying manuscripts, publishing music, paying royalties to singers, and advertising.

The pirates form a limited company.

The battle against piracy is expensive.

Mr. T. P. O'Connor takes charge of the new copyright bill.

The Yorkshire Post *sides with the pirates, argues with the musicsellers.*

A Musical Defence League forms.

15 November 1903

MUSIC PIRACIES IN THE PROVINCES.

CIRCULAR BY THE MUSIC PUBLISHERS' ASSOCIATION.

THE following circular was issued last month by the Music Publishers' Association to the music dealers of the provinces:—

The Music Publishers' Association,
27, Regent Street, London, S.W.
October 9th, 1903.

DEAR SIRS,

Re Music Piracies.

In consequence of the continued traffic in music piracies, especially in the provinces, it has been decided by the Music Publishers' Association to take similar steps to those adopted by the Musical Copyright Association, and for this purpose we are compelled to solicit your immediate and active co-operation.

Until the present unsatisfactory state of the law in connexion with musical copyright can be remedied, it is absolutely imperative that all interested in the music trade should join forces and use every means to keep in check as far as possible the trade in pirate reprints. To this end you are invited to communicate whenever possible with the Music Publishers' Association, who will give you every assistance in their power.

In certain towns and districts a great deal has already been accomplished through the personal attention of members of the trade, and we trust you will be willing to join us, and so extend the scope of our operations.

We shall be pleased to hear from you and give you advice and instructions how to act in the seizure of piracies. We have now ready the necessary forms of authorization, and a supply will be sent you immediately upon application.

We are yours faithfully,

BOOSEY & CO.
CHAPPELL & CO., LTD. } Sub-Committee for dealing with Music Piracies.

L&PMTR, p. 21[160]

160. *No copy of the original found (see 'Missing Documents', Appendix, pp.143–4).*

December 1903

The insufficiency of the present laws is pointed up in a case prosecuted in Liverpool for the Music Publishers' Association by its agent, Mr. Arthur Preston. Armed with a warrant, Mr. Preston and a policeman had seized nearly 200 illegal copies on the street. With further authorization he and three detectives subsequently raided premises 'occupied by one So-an-So' seizing another 7,000 copies. In court the following day, the magistrate's clerk asked for proof that the music seized at the house had been offered for sale. Mr. Preston and associates were unable to convince the court that they were there to be sold—and 'it was even urged that the copies be returned to the defendant!' The bench, however, decided they should be destroyed. *MO&MTR*, p. 233

The Musicsellers Association meets again in Bradford to discuss pricing policies and ways to induce London firms to join them. *ibid.*

In the provinces, Francis, Day & Hunter's sixpenny songs are a foremost topic with dealers. Already 'outsiders' are further cutting prices to 4d. or 3 copies for 1s. and dealers are left in a state of unrest and uncertainty. *ibid.*

'Argus', a provincial correspondent, notes a falling off in trade for the pirates. They are now asking fourpence for their copies, and 'they have strangled their own trade by doubling their prices'. *MO&MTR*, pp. 233-34

January 1904

'Berners' [obviously a dealer] writes about 'Pirates and Prices', commenting that the cutting of prices by publishers has been as serious to dealers 'as is piracy at present for the publishers'. To avoid some difficulties he suggests that music publishers adopt the procedures of the book publishers: issue sheets at the price they wish them to be retailed and insist on musicsellers adhering to this price 'on pain of having their supplies cut off'. *MO&MTR*, pp. 318–19

Mr. W. J. Galloway, M.P., will soon introduce a new bill dealing with musical piracy designed to meet the objections raised to the Musical Copyright Bill of last year. [Elsewhere Mr. James Caldwell, M.P., is accused of obstructing that corrective legislation as well as making the earlier Act of 1902 ineffective.] Where identification of persons engaged in the printing and dissemination of pirated music has been possible, it has been ascertained that they 'are alien Jews'. *MO&MTR*, p. 323

February 1904

Letters continue to pour in from dealers voicing discontent with the trade practices of publishers. 'Disgusted Retailer', who is turning to the piano trade, thinks 'Now that the publisher is in his death grapple with the pirates perhaps he will have some feeling for the retail musicseller . . . Piracy has been a blessing to me, because ever since it commenced I have not had half so much work to do for nothing'.

'Country Dealer' finds his clan caught between the publisher and the pirate, 'between the devil and the deep sea', and recounts many of the difficulties with discounts, travellers, and with arrogant treatment by the publishers—complaints repeatedly voiced to the *MO&MTR* for the past dozen years. He notes the case of a dealer nearly mobbed, his shop nearly wrecked, for 'tackling pirate hawkers' in the name of the Music Publishers' Association, whose orders—a few days later to a member of that association—were shabbily treated.

Four other letters in the same issue echo many of these feelings.

MO&MTR, pp. 393–94

In a London police court, Mr. Rutland prosecutes another case concerning some 73,988 pirated copies seized in one location. The magistrate's decision is to destroy all but 200 copies (where the ownership of the copyright is in question) and levy costs of ten guineas, which is paid. *MO&MTR*, p. 396

April 1904

'Music Publishers and Parliament' reprinted from *The Times*, reviews the copyright laws before and after the Act of 1902, the shortcomings of those which now prevail, and various unsatisfactory judicial interpretations of them. A new bill introduced into the House of Commons by Mr. Mount 'appears fairly to meet the principal necessities of the case'. Mr. Caldwell, who has worked successfully against improvements in past sessions, has submitted a minority report maintaining that copyright in music is artificial ownership brought about by legislation, not natural justice. He has excused the pirates for their activities because of the high prices charged for music by its legitimate owners. The *MO&MTR* believes, however, that in hearing arguments, it is regrettable 'that the committee did not feel justified in requesting publishers to disclose detailed accounts of their business', but pronounced themselves satisfied that the publishers' costs were heavy.[161]

MO&MTR, p. 558

161. *James Caldwell, M. P., was one member of a Home Department Committee appointed to study the need for changes in the copyright law. Among those giving evidence to the Committee were the publishers Boosey, Day, and Enoch; the composers Monckton and Maybrick; Arthur Preston, the MPA's pirate hunter; and Frederick Willetts, known as 'Fisher, the King of the Pirates', who volunteered to testify.* (Min. Bk., *295v*). *The official account is in the Home Department's* Report of the Departmental Committee on Piracy of Musical Publications *(Parliamentary Papers, v. 79, pp. 277–381).*

In Liverpool, Messrs. Wishert and Meyer, agents of the Music Publishers' Association, and a detective armed with a warrant seized 2,500 pirated editions from a music dealer who is fined two guineas for having the copies and for supplying them to hawkers. The selling of illegal copies goes on but recent prosecutions have forced hawkers to work more in residential areas. There, 'at the rear of houses', copies 'are being shouted as lustily as the evening papers'. *MO&MTR*, p. 559

Chappell & Co., in a brief letter, indicate that if Mr. Caldwell's proposed amendments to the new bill are accepted, the new law will be as impotent as the old. *ibid.*

May 1904

Francis, Day & Hunter win an action for infringement of copyright against the printers A. J. Childe and his father, James Childe, of Islington. With the magistrate's order for seizure in hand, some 9,000 illegal copies were taken from the firm. Mr. Day testified that the cheapest way to produce pirated copies was by 'photo zinc blocks. After the outlay for production of the blocks (which must cost eleven shillings) the copies could be turned out at a halfpenny each'. The defendants' firm was turning out about 5,000 pirated copies a day. The father testified that though he knew his son had a quantity of music stored on the premises, and though he had paid the hire of a machine he knew was used to print pirated music, 'he had nothing to do with the printing of it'.

The magistrate fined both defendants £100 and granted an injunction against the firm.[162] *MO&MTR*, pp. 635–36

162. *Reported earlier in the* Islington Morning Advertiser *for 18 March 1904 (clipping is preserved in Arthur Preston's* Clipping Book, *in the British Library, pressmark M. 55. See note at December 1905.)*

June 1904

'Progress' sends a clipping from the *Daily Telegraph* containing some remarks made by Mr. D'Eyncourt, magistrate of the Clerkenwell Police Court, while hearing arguments for an order for seizure. 'I wonder the music publishers who hold copyrights do not reduce their price. With the growing taste in music, the demand is very great . . . [as] the enormous amount of this pirated music shows'.

'Progress' compliments the new, legitimate sixpenny editions and wonders why 'If one publisher can do it, why should not others?' And if the publishers would eliminate the agents following pirates all over Britain, the costs of moving the law courts, and the royalties paid singers, 'Progress' thinks they could all sell music cheap. *MO&MTR*, pp. 711–12

'Opinion' thinks the principal problem is travellers' terms. *MO&MTR*, p. 712

15 June 1904

> The latest seizure, made early this month, by the Music Publishers' Association reaches the astonishing figure of 109,698 copies. The taste of the "pirates'" public says the "Express," is curiously mixed, if the stock found on their premises is a safe guide. For instance 150 copies of 'Queen of the Earth' were held sufficient to supply the demand for that. Mr. German's three dances survive even the barrel organs, the desperate "pirate" had 2,625 copies of them in stock. 'Cavalleria Rusticana,' is strong, for there were 2,560 copies on hand, but 'A Chinese Honeymoon' was stronger, with a score of 2,660. There were 700 copies of 'The John Bull Store.' The following list will show what other melodies are in popular demand. 'Everybody's loved by someone,' 1,900; 'The Belle of New York,' 1,800; 'The Holy City,' 1,800; 'Because I love you,' 1,600; 'Sammy,' 1,450; 'Abide with me,' 1,400; 'The Boers have got my daddy,' 1,250; 'Honeysuckle and the Bee,' 1,100; 'It's nice to have a home of your own,' 1,010; 'She ain't a bit like the other gals,' 1,000; 'She is a sensible girl,' 700; 'Sunshine and Rain,' 600; 'Star of my Soul,' 600; 'Tell me, pretty maiden,' 600; 'Pansy Faces,' 500; 'Try again, Johnnie,' 450; 'What is the use of loving a girl?' 425.

L&PMTR, p. 238

July 1904

The new copyright bill, as amended by the standing committee, is considered by the House of Commons on 10 June. Mr. Caldwell and a number of his supporters call for repeated readings of certain clauses and propose many amendments in an attempt to delay and lessen the effectiveness of the act. The first lengthy arguments and suggested changes are to do with compulsory registration within a certain period of time after publication. Mr. Atherley, one of Mr. Caldwell's supporters, proposes a clause allowing courts to refuse to grant warrants or levy fines unless 'it was satisfied that the reasonable requirements of the public [i.e., cheap prices] had been satisfied'. Mr. Harwood feels the prices of music are prohibitive . . . The rights of the public must be considered'.

Mr. H. D. Greene declares that he is humiliated at the treatment of the law by both sides. He finds preposterous the idea that, though a defendant in a piracy case might be found guilty, the magistrate would have to let him go free 'if some want of the public was not satisfied'. Who is to decide that?

Mr. Caldwell, stating that the bill would give music copyright holders dramatic powers not possessed by owners of any other kind, insists that the requirements of the public must be satisfied. Mr. Harwood lays the blame for 'the disease' for which the House is being asked to find a cure 'in the fact that the whole trade of music publishing [is] rotten . . . in fact one of the most outrageous examples of a trust'. In view of the absurd prices of music, piracy is inevitable.

Major Seeley finally speaks for the composers, noting that they are among the principal sufferers and that for every one publisher hurt by the pirates there are dozens of unfortunate composers.

Mr. Weir sympathizes with the composers, but the publishers are to blame.

Another resolution by Mr. Caldwell to omit Subsection II draws no response from the promoters of the bill, and Mr. Warner notes that either the amendment is important or it is not, but either way, the promoters should express some opinion on it. There is little, but the vote is decidedly against the Caldwell amendment.

Mr. Caldwell is moving another amendment when adjournment is called for. *MO&MTR*, pp. 788–89

A series of replies by William Boosey to 'mis-statements' contained in something called Mr. Caldwell's 'Memorandum' is printed in full.[163]

1) The present bill is promoted by the Musical Copyright Association. *Boosey's answer:* no.

2) No composers were called to testify. *Boosey:* Two were.

3) The committee discovered that the interest of the public in cheap music had not been provided for. *Boosey:* Catalogues of classical and popular music at 2d. a copy by numerous publishers have been in existence for fifty years.

4) The acts of 1882 and 1888 were passed to restrict the arbitrary rights of publishers. *Boosey:* They were passed on the initiative of the publishers themselves to protect the public from vexatious proceedings for performing fees brought against them by Mr. Henry Wall. The acts required that notice of performance fees be printed on the title page.

5) Pirates have recognized 'to the fullest the rights of authors and composers in the law'. *Boosey:* Nonsense. Every piracy is a direct robbery of the composer's property.

6) Music copyright owners enjoy the same protections and remedies as book owners. *Boosey:* No. It is easier to pirate sheet music than a large book.

7) The price of music compares unfavourably with the price of books. *Boosey:* A 6s. novel is read once and cast aside; a new song at one and fourpence can be in daily use for months or longer. A complete vocal score of a comic opera, two to three hundred pages,

163. *Seven major points of Caldwell's 'Memorandum' (or 'Manifesto', as it is called elsewhere; see here Sept. 1905) are summarized in the* L&PMTR *for 15 June 1904 (p. 29) along with 'The Third Reading Debate'. Though printed and known to have been circulated, no copies of Caldwell's document have been found (see 'Missing Documents', Appendix, pp. 143–4).*

costs four and six to six shillings.

8) The price for copyright music is excessive considering the costs. *Boosey:* All of these must make a living from it—author, composer, singers, publisher and staff, paper maker, printer, and retailer.

9) The present situation is caused by the great and ever increasing market for music. *Boosey:* There will always be a great and increasing market for stolen goods sold with impunity at less than cost.

10) The cost of production is only a few shillings for an edition of 1,000 copies. *Boosey:* Yes, if applied to the 'filthy and unhealthy paper upon which pirated editions are issued'.

11) Composers never receive more than one penny to twopence halfpenny per copy royalty. *Boosey:* They very rarely receive less than threepence a copy, sometimes as much as 6d., besides other fees.

12) The case of Piccolomini's extraordinarily popular *Ora Pro Nobis*, for which he was paid only £10, instances what happens in the publishing world. *Boosey:* Piccolomini has again and again received large sums for songs that were failures.

13) Payments to singers and for advertising are not part of production costs. *Boosey:* Such often result in a dead loss; they do not necessarily force a sale.

14) Retailers make a profit of 1s to 1s 1p on copyright music sold to the public. *Boosey:* They are lucky if they make from 2d. to 4d. a copy. The pirates have ruined what business they had, even at that return.

15) Music is sold to the public at the marked price of 4s. *Boosey:* Most publishers have long since marked their sheet music 2s. and not 4s.

16) Professors and teachers buy from retailers at 1s. and sell to their students at 4s. *Boosey:* A scandalous mis-statement! A profit of 3s?!

17) Stores receive better terms from music publishers than do the retailers. *Boosey:* Precisely the same terms.

18) Day's sixpenny editions show that piracy can be suppressed by issuing cheap editions. *Boosey:* Mr. Day's sixpenny edition has, itself, been pirated left and right, sold wholesale in the streets.

19) Mr. D'Eyncourt's statements that publishers, for not selling music cheaper, are responsible for piracies, proves Mr. Caldwell's contentions. *Boosey:* The piracy of Mr. Day's sixpenny editions is exclusive evidence to the contrary.

20) If a song does not satisfy a high standard of taste it is disqualified from proper copyright protection. *Boosey:* Would you protect only calico of superior quality from stealing?[164]

21) The public does not know whether a piece of music is copyright or not. *Boosey:* Every copyright piece bears the word 'copyright' on its title as well as the first year of publication in this country.

22) Successful copyright music only enjoys a sale of a few months, at most a year or two. *Boosey:* All the more reason—if true—to give it

164. *Mr. Caldwell is a wealthy calico manufacturer from Glasgow. See Boosey's comments below, August 1904.*

the fullest protection.

23) Copyright is only a privilege, not property. *Boosey:* This is 'twaddle', that a man is entitled to less protection for the work of his brain (his composition) than for the work of his hands (e.g., a watch).

MO&MTR, pp. 789–90

August 1904

A 'Great Protest Meeting at Queen's Hall', under the auspices of a new Musical Defence League, takes place on 4 July. The Duke of Argyll presides, supported by the Hon. Harry Lawson, M.P.'s Galloway, Mount, and Malcolm, Sir Edward Elgar, Sir Hubert Parry, Dr. F. H. Cowen, Messrs. John Murray, Stephen Adams, T. E. Scrutton, F. E. Weatherly, J. Herbert Marshall, J.P. (President of the Provincial Music Trades Association), and others.

The Duke starts with a stirring commentary on the rights of composers and the acts of the pirates—punctuated with cheers from the assemblage. He has been told that in just three years, three million copies have been seized. He hopes the new bill will be passed this session.

William Boosey then reads letters of apology and sympathy from Lords Knutsford, Lytton, and Latham, M.P.s Gladstone, O'Connor, and Wortley, from Sir Arthur Conan Doyle, Sir Charles Villiers Stanford, Mr. Rudyard Kipling, and many others.

Most of their letters vehemently assert the need for the provisions of the new bill, and their remarks, as they are read, evoke cheers. A long review of the past and present copyright situations by Mr. David Day begins with the words, 'Down with the Pirates!' followed by cheering.

In the final talk, Mr. William Boosey recounts Mr. Caldwell's legislative activities and reflects on the man himself. When the 1902 bill was passing through the House, he says, Mr. Caldwell 'made the discovery that the pirates were a very deserving class of people', deserving of parliamentary protection, and that composers and their associates are pariahs and outcasts. He set to work and rendered the 1902 bill useless and inoperative. He also opposed and pulled to pieces the 1903 bill under the pretext that it ignored the rights of the pirates. On one condition he would have accepted it: that for nine months after passage, pirates would be allowed to print and sell copies, and that copies printed during that time would not be liable to later confiscation and penalty. 'His obstructive tactics' are a scandal 'without equal or precedent in parliamentary history'.

Mr. Caldwell is a very wealthy calico manufacturer and real estate owner from Glasgow, and Boosey asks why it is wicked to make money by printing music on paper and not wicked to print patterns on calico. If Mr. Caldwell believes cheap music is a necessity for the poorer classes, should he not consider cheap, or even free, calico for them too? Does he give the use of his real estate free to tenants of the poorer classes? (Cheers and laughter.)

Mr. Boosey rejoices in the fact that the new bill 'has been given first place in the ballot' in the House and is pleased with the organization which has been called into existence by this meeting. (Cheers.) Musicians deserve mutual defence. (Hear, hear.) The association will have agents in every town and corner of this country. 'Eventually truth and justice do prevail amongst us'. (Hear, hear.) 'Our appeal will not be in vain'. (Loud cheers.) *MO&MTR*, pp. 861–63

October 1904

'The Copyright Scandal', reprinted from *Truth*, notes another effect of the piracies. To keep good faith with composers, to avoid the possibility that one of their new works might prove popular enough for the pirates to drain off all legitimate sales, publishers are now responding to writers with printed forms such as this: 'Messrs. Chappell & Co. regret to inform M ... They are unable to purchase or publish any more musical compositions until musical property is adequately protected by act of parliament. They return the accompanying manuscript with best thanks for the offer of the same'. A similar printed form is being sent to singers about programme fees.[165]

The monetary losses to the pirates have been astounding. Recently Messrs. Chappell & Co. 'made a haul of over one hundred thousand copies of a single work', one of *The Cingalee* arrangements. It is heartening to learn that the new Musical Defence League intends to press in every possible way for remedial legislation.[166]

Meanwhile the public is not blameless; anyone who buys from the purveyors of stolen property becomes an accessory after the fact to downright robbery. Those who, if offered a stolen ring or watch of doubtful origin would probably send for a policeman, 'will cheerfully purchase a copy of *The Holy City* or *Ora Pro Nobis*, and indignantly repudiate the suggestion that they are doing a shabby thing'. *MO&MTR*, pp. 62–63

165. *No copy of either of these documents has been found (see 'Missing Documents', Appendix, pp. 143–4).*

166. *The Musical Defence League was composed of music publishers, composers—among them Ivan Caryll, Edward Elgar, Edward German—and others, such as W. H. Cummings. See more here at Feb. 1905 and 30 June 1905.*

December 1904

A writer calling himself 'The Wanderer' states that 'the more open and unblushing forms of sheet music piracy have disappeared from some northern towns', but fresh problems have arisen. There is an entirely new trade to deal with; shops for the sale of very cheap music are springing up all over. Cheap music selling at 2d. or 3d. per copy is now stocked by tradesmen who have never previously had anything to do with the music business. And 'the gutter merchants still remain'.

Musicsellers must accommodate the fact that the mind of the public is now set on cheap music. There are cheap shilling and sixpence albums with selections of good music, large shilling folios and albums with much first class, though old, music, and an enormous range of classical music offered in the Augener, Peters, and other editions. There are also, of course, extensive catalogues of well-printed, non-copyright pieces. Looking at this mass of good music available in cheap editions, one wonders 'that so much comparatively high-priced, copyright sheet music should still be sold . . . The era of cheap music has begun'.

MO&MTR, p. 221

January 1905

From the *Daily Mail*: 'Are we on the eve of a revolution in the publication of music?' In 1870 the ordinary song or ballad was published at 4s. by 1900 at 2s. from 1904 onward for 6d or less. The music loving public has the music pirate to thank. It is estimated that over two million pirated copies of *The Holy City* and one million of *In Old Madrid* have been sold—and a further two million seized and destroyed in just the last twelve months!

MO&MTR, pp. 296–97

Messrs. Chappell & Co. respond vigorously: 'It is unfortunate that the *Daily Mail* can find no better way to advertise their new editions of sixpenny songs' than an article glorifying the pirate. High prices did not create the pirates, the indifference of government did.

Chappell notes that earlier, similar undertakings by newspapers—the *Strand Musical Magazine*, and *Melody*, published by the *Daily Express*—each gave buyers six or eight new copyright songs for 6d, but they have all long since ceased to exist. After some ironic admonitions, he wishes the *Daily Mail* good fortune and urges it—for its own protection—to join others who are attempting to get a new copyright bill. *MO&MTR*, p. 297

February 1905

Commercial travellers, representing nearly every music publishing house, meet on 7 January in London to discuss the harm done to them and the trade in general by the pirates and to approve a letter setting out their views on current legislation which is to be sent to Mr. Balfour, M.P. In a review of the problems, the Chairman, Mr. J. Jenning of Boosey & Co., notes a seizure in Hackney in October of 237,718 illegal copies, among them upwards of thirty songs and pieces which could have been bought in legitimate editions for sixpence. High price, therefore, is not an important factor that warrants discussion; 'however cheap the published price of music, it [will be] taken up by the pirates and reproduced at a lower rate'.

The committee drafting the letter has sought help from and an alliance with the United Kingdom Commercial Travellers Association, an organization of some 30,000 members. (Hear, hear.)

The letter to Mr. Balfour is read and unanimously approved, and discussion moves to a second resolution which asks the committee of the U.K. Commercial Travellers' Association for its help in obtaining an interview with Mr. Caldwell. 'If they could only get into a room with Mr. Caldwell for half an hour or less (Laughter) they would be fully able to convince him that he had not acted well'. If that meeting comes about, Mr. Caldwell will be certain to bring up the issue of high prices, because it is this argument which has gained him all he sought and has, in fact, caused a reduction in prices.

The Chairman hopes they will be able to arrange a meeting with the musicsellers. The music printers are 'already moving, and also the music engravers'. Mr. Smith suggests an appeal to organizations such as the Incorporated Society of Musicians, the Royal Society of Musicians, the Royal College of Music, and the Royal Academy of Music, but the Chairman points out that there is a Musical Defence League supported by these bodies which ought to be making its own representations on the question.

MO&MTR, pp. 374–75

March 1905

Mr. Gerald Balfour, M.P., President of the Board of Trade, receives a deputation from the Leeds Musicsellers' Association and promises them his support for the new legislation in the House. In the conversation the Association calls his attention to the recent seizure of 247,000 copies weighing between four and five tons.

MO&MTR, p. 452

An article from *Truth* says that publishers in the Midlands are thankful for a seven-year sentence recently imposed at Birmingham on one Evans. While this was not for his work as a pirate but for other crimes, those who have long sought to stop his distribution of piracies are pleased. He has frustrated attempts to seize copies for years, for though the right to search can be obtained, it does not carry with it authorization to effect forcible entry. One day, in Mr. Evan's absence, the police 'obtained admission to the pirate's lair', and found there, in addition to several hundred thousands of illegally produced copies of music, the proceeds of numerous burglaries. These, not the piracies, are what have sent him to jail.

The usual difficulty of obtaining admission without forcing the door resulted in a comic situation in South London. While the pirates were kept beleaguered in one part of the building by a make-believe 'frontal' attack, without their knowing it, the whole of the 'swag' was removed through a skylight at the back of the house. Amusing this may be for some, says *Truth*, but it is very serious for those 'whose property is the subject of these Homeric conflicts', and it urges quick passage of the 'brief and absolutely noncontentious' measure in the House. *MO&MTR*, p. 456

From 'Trade Jottings': 'Last month a limited company was formed to carry on the business of musical piracy. The police and agents of the Musical Copyright and Publishers Associations marked its inauguration by seizing two vanloads of pirated music, estimated at 1,500 copies, from one of the company's depots in Walworth'. One day last month the same group visited a warehouse in Latham Junction and seized over a quarter of a million pirated copies. *MO&MTR*, p. 462

April 1905

A meeting of the Master Music Printers' Association was held last month at Queen's Hall. A letter to Mr. Balfour urging passage of the new bill was approved. It includes a request that he receive a deputation from the group. *MO&MTR*, p. 540

May 1905

Mr. J. E. Strong, Chairman of the Master Music Printers Association, tells the *MO&MTR*, 'What we want is a short bill of one clause imposing a fine of 1s per copy on any person found printing or offering for sale pirated music, with imprisonment in default.' Those struggling against the pirates, he says, are powerless; when a printer of pirated music is run down, 'he is invariably a man of straw'. During February alone, more than a million copies were seized from them, but none were put out of business. In London, the copies are printed chiefly in the East End, but plates are duplicated and sent 'wherever a shady small printer is to be found'. Printers who have invested in large plants for printing copyright music will be in poor condition now that the publishers have decided not to publish any more. *MO&MTR*, pp. 614–15

At meetings of the Music Publishers' Association on 7 and 13 April,[167] thirty-seven of the largest and best known music publishers sign a declaration stating that until they are given legislative protection from music piracies: 1) no further new publications will be issued; 2) no fresh contracts for payments to artists and singers will be entered into; and 3) no further money will be spent upon newspaper advertisements. The signers include Ashdown, Boosey,

167. Min. Bk., *298v–300*.

Bosworth, Chappell, Cramer, Donajowski, Enoch, Gould, Hawkes, Church, Prowse, Metzler, Ricordi, Witmark, and others. Novello, Breitkopf & Härtel, Augener, and Schott express sympathy with statement number one and will cooperate fully with numbers two and three.[168] *MO&MTR*, p. 615

Mr. Balfour, M.P., who was formally thanked for his support by the Music Publishers' Association at their last meeting,[169] is asked by Sir Andrew Agnew in the House of Commons if Balfour has heard that the publishers have quit publishing new music. Balfour has seen the statement and thinks it a case of hardship. 'But when my hon. friend asks me to take up a private member's bill, I see great difficulties in the way. I would much prefer bringing forward a government measure . . . I cannot give any pledge on the subject'. *ibid.*

The parliamentary correspondent of the *Daily Telegraph* believes legislation on musical piracy will be gotten through this season. The 'opposition has been reduced to almost vanishing point'; even Mr. Caldwell admits that something must be done. It will probably be a one-clause, noncontentious, government measure. *MO&MTR*, p. 616

A long article about 'The Position of the Publishers', reprinted from the *Daily Telegraph*, sums up the sorry state of the music trade, now climaxed by the publishers' decision to cease publishing. 'Mr. Caldwell's triumph is all but complete'. Though pirates may not now be rampant in central London, they are everywhere in the suburbs and provinces. The Music Publishers' Association and the Musical Copyright Association have spent thousand of pounds attempting to get their stocks destroyed.

From the minutes of the Annual General Meeting of the Music Publishers' Association, June 1905:

ANALYSIS OF PIRACY EXPENDITURE ACCOUNT TO 31st MAY, 1905.

	£	s.	d.
Solicitors' Fees after deducting Costs recovered	249	7	10
Provincial Agents' Expenses (travelling, &c.)...	296	12	11
London Agents' Expenses (travelling, police, &c.)	320	7	4
Wages to Regular Agents in London and Provinces	702	18	6
Allowances to Volunteer Agents in London and Provinces	187	19	4
Cash in Cooper's hands...	7	4	9
	£1,764	10	8

168. *Despite their proclamations of doom, publishers apparently expected to realize comfortable profits, even from pieces which were being mercilessly and continually pirated. Why else would they pay enormous prices for such copyrights and plates at auction like those in Puttick & Simpson's sale of H. Beresford's copyrights on 18 and 19 May 1905? In this, the same month in which the publishers announced they would cease publishing, the following prices were paid for a number of ceaselessly pirated songs:*

- Big Ben *by Pontet, bought by Tuckwood for £231.*
- Gladiator *by J. H. Adams, bought by Ashdown for £178.*
- Last Milestone *by Pontet, bought by Tuckwood for £531.*
- Oh! Hear *by Mattei, bought by Tuckwood for £513.*
- Skipper *by Jude, bought by Ashdown for £570.*
- Gigue in C *by Watson, bought by Donajowski for £324.*

It will be remembered that Ashdown was one of the leaders of the move to cease publishing!

169. *Gerald Balfour's heightened interest in a new copyright bill may have had something to do with his brother's experience with pirates around this time. As William Boosey recounts in his* Fifty Years of Music *(London: Ernest Benn Ltd., 1931), pp. 116–17, Arthur James Balfour, then Prime Minister, had just published a little treatise,* Economic Notes on Insular Free Trade *(New York, London: Longmans Green, 1903) at one shilling. 'Suddenly a pirated copy . . . appeared on the streets retailing at one penny', with a note from the pirate editor stating that the work was of such great educational value it was necessary to bring it within the reach of the masses!*

For more about the two brothers, see 'Dramatis Personae', p. 3.

In London, the last three seizures of illegal copies amounted to a total near 700,000 copies, collected within a couple of weeks. The *Telegraph* quotes Mr. Boosey on what is needed: a short bill to amend the Act of 1902 adding a nominal penalty of 1s. per printed copy, in default, imprisonment. The paper supports the legislation.
MO&MTR, p. 616

The publishers have taken an unprecedented step by refusing to publish because 'parliament does not stir. Nothing more pitiably and incredibly foolish ever occurred than the attempt to pass a short bill dealing with this subject. All that had to be done was to interpret piracy as theft. And what occurred? Mr. Galloway takes charge of the bill; Mr. Caldwell, for reasons of his own, blocks it,—and there's the end of it'.[170] A short bill, taking five minutes to draft, would put a stop to the whole business, says the angry *MO&MTR*, but parliament chatters, argues, squabbles, fights and waste time on a matter where there is wide agreement, a matter wholly removed from party debate. The public agrees with Mercutio: 'A plague on both your houses'.
MO&MTR, pp. 616–17

170. *At a meeting of the Music Publishers' Association 'and the Music Trade' on 5 May 1905, William Boosey reported that T. P. O'Connor, M.P., has come forward volunteering to approach Caldwell urging him to drop his opposition. If that fails he will work to get the Government to bring forward a Government Bill.*

June 1905

The *Daily Chronicle* points out some ancient history. In 1691 'the number of hawkers and pedlars greatly interfering with the retail trade of the city', an act of Common Council was passed imposing on both seller and buyer a penalty of 40 shillings for trading in the street. When the trade moved off the streets into the markets, another act was passed. *MO&MTR*, p. 621

Mr. T. P. O'Connor has taken charge of the bill in the House and has interviewed Mr. Caldwell in an attempt to change his views. In case it is decided that the bill should be a government measure, a different bill is being readied.

The Council of the London Chamber of Commerce passes a very strong resolution in support of the legislation. It is to be sent to the Prime Minister and all members of Parliament belonging to the Chamber. Sir Albert Rollit will see Mr. Caldwell to find a basis for settlement. *MO&MTR*, p. 691

30 June 1905

[In the MPA *Minute Book* are three documents of this date dealing with 'an important meeting of the principal Musical Composers and Music Publishers . . . held at Queen's Hall on Thursday last, 29th inst. under the Chairmanship of Sir Alexander Mackenzie'.

The subject was musical copyright. One of the documents is on the letterhead of the Musical Defence League. The other two list composers and publishers in attendance, among whom were: (composers) Ivan Caryll, Madame Guy d'Hardelot, Miss Emily Clarke, Miss Teresa del Riego, Edward German, W. E. Imeson, Gerald Lane, Tito Mattei, Hubert Parry, Leslie Stuart, Sir Edward Elgar, Sir Charles Villiers Stanford, Dr. F. H. Cowen, and Paolo Tosti. The publishers included Ascherberg, Ashdown, Augener, Boosey, Bosworth, Broome, Cramer, and thirty-two others.

Another meeting of the Defence League was held on 17 July with, in general, the same persons attending. Reports about the progress of the Copyright Bill through 'a moribund House' of Commons were all gloomy. The consensus is to try again, next session.] MPA *Min. Bk.* between 309 and 310

August 1905

A bankruptcy examination in Leeds and an argument over its causes emphasize the seriousness of the piracy assault and reveals the naiveté of some of the public.

Mr. William Elliott is in bankruptcy court because he has over-extended himself by laying in heavy stocks and moving to more expensive premises. 'We could not foresee the pirate business lasting so long . . . We have done all we could. We have petitioned every member of Parliament; and the King has been approached'. Abruptly, at this point, the examination is adjourned.

Letters begin to appear in the *Yorkshire Post* about the case. The first, from a representative of the Leeds Musicsellers' Association, reviews the events leading up to the present and notes special problems in Leeds where the stipendiary magistrate holds that to impose a fine under the guise of costs on a guilty pirate strains the law. As an example of the result, a pirate from whose premises 900 copies were seized a few months ago, resumed operations almost immediately and now issues a catalogue offering 500 different piracies for sale. The need for the proposed new legislation is reasserted.

In a disagreeable tone of voice the *Post* comments on the letter. Why should the public bear the cost of protecting the owners of musical copyright when they do not do so for other copyright owners. It is improper to make infringement of one class of copyright criminal without dealing similarly with all.

The first writer tries to describe to the *Post* the magnitude of the problem, the differences between infringement of copyright on hundreds of three- to four-page sheets and on a handful of 300- to 400-page novels. He points out that 'three quarter of a million copies of pirated music were seized in the first 2 months of this year alone', yet the illegal traffic slowed not a whit. Pirates of copyrighted material other than music generally must be persons of means to do so; the pirates of music, on the other hand, are 'men of straw with no fixed abodes'. Injunctions, damages, and costs deter them not at all. Bankruptcies of musicsellers are happening at an increasing and alarming rate.

The *Post* responds that 'publishers of novels are alive to the facts, and if they wish to catch the public they issue at a popular price'. The musicsellers should force the publishers to do the same; it is a remedy they have not tried.

From the musicseller: Music dealers are in favour of cheap prices, too; but the law does not encourage the issuance of cheap editions. No sooner does music 'catch on', whether published at 1s. 6d. or at 6d., than it is pirated. One firm has issued 147 pieces at 6d., and already at least fifty of those have been pirated. Cheap music is not a way of meeting the pirates on their own ground.

The *Post:* If legitimate sales of printed editions are on this very large scale, then 'sixpence is not a low price but a high one. There was much cheaper music printed sixty years ago'. The publishers should try selling music 'really cheap'. No special protective legislation should be passed for them. *MO&MTR*, p. 830

'With a feeling of long pent relief . . . all have observed the introduction', by the Hon. T. H. Cochrane, and first reading of a musical copyright bill. It will surely be amended but, as it is, it offers some comfort. There are penalties, the maximum restricted to £20, which is not an amount to deter the larger pirates, but the cumulative fine of 1s. per copy ought to deter the average stock holder and street hawker. The *MO&MTR* is both puzzled and amused that the operation of the search warrant is confined to 'office hours!'

MO&MTR, p. 831

A west coast music dealer protests that 'Publishers themselves have contributed to the spoiling of the Egyptians . . .' If a dealer desires a certain piece, why is he compelled to take half a dozen that he does not want? 'I would not raise my finger to help any of the big publishers. Why should I? They charge me 1s. and 4d. for a piece that they know I cannot get more for than 18d. after carriage'.

It is clear to the reporter that musicsellers are out of sympathy with the publishers, indifferent to the fight between them and the pirates. The dealers know they are also hurt by the pirates, but they do not feel the publishers have done anything to protect the retailers' interests in their struggle. *MO&MTR*, p. 833

[For a number of years, under the rubric, 'Prominent Music Publishers', the *MO&MTR* has run a series of lengthy articles describing leading music publishing firms. In this issue, the feature is:]

'X.—Pirates Unlimited. This concern—an unchartered and unincorporated company—is not by any means of modern origin'. There follows a summary of the history of musical copyright, the legislation respecting it and a review of landmark decisions going all the way back to Bach vs. Longman in 1777. Today, piracy is much more extensive and ruinous due to modern machinery and cheaper production methods. On Monday, 17 July past, for example, 287,792 pirated copies were seized at one distribution point in Dalston,[171] a fraud that represents a wholesale robbery of nearly £15,000. *MO&MTR*, pp. 383–84

171. *The 'Press Cuttings' book belonging to Arthur Preston, principal agent for the MPA [see note 176 at December 1905] contains a clipping from an unidentified newspaper dated 17 July 1905 which notes other details of the 'Dalston Raid': in some stables, a little way from the main road, 'police found no fewer than 4,000,000 copies of music, as well as fine printing machines'. In a later court case of the culprit, G. Wooton, the count was given as 287,792.*

September 1905

Within three weeks in early August no less than half a million copies of pirated music and £500 worth of plates have been seized in London from pirates preparing for the autumn season. These captures comprised the following:

17 July—287,790 copies seized at a temporary warehouse in Bentley Road belonging to George Wooton.[172] He did not appear in court. The music was ordered destroyed, and Wooton was fined ten guineas. On the 22nd, the defendant in default was sentenced to one month in jail.

172. *Cf. note 171.*

4 August—another group of 6,489 copies were seized—almost all copies of Boosey copyrights—at the premises of Miss Gothubena Martin of Devons Road.[173]

173. *A lengthy report of this raid was carried in the* London Telegraph *for 16 August 1905.*

10 August—seizure of 150,000 copies was effected at Eden Grove, Upper Holloway, 'known to be the lair of some of the newest and smartest printers of "the stuff"'.

17 August—From premises at Cazenove Yard, a seizure was made of at least 50,000 copies and a large number of pirated plates.[174] *MO&MTR*, p. 960B

174. *Also in the* London Telegraph.

Mr. Charles A. Lucas, Secretary of the Royal Society of Musicians of Great Britain writes the editor: 'It may interest you to know that Mr. Caldwell has lately issued a manifesto of four pages of printed foolscap to justify his action in opposing the musical copyright act'. He has scattered it broadcast—in view of the forthcoming general election—and the pirates have seized upon this weapon; one is said to have distributed 1,000 copies to his customers.[175] *ibid.*

175. *As indicated earlier, no copies of the original of this 'Manifesto' have been found. See 'Missing Documents', Appendix, pp. 143-4).*

December 1905—The end

The publishers try a new stratagem.

The 'Great Prosecution for Conspiracy' begins—the beginning of the end.

The 'King of the Pirates' and cohorts face justice.

Willets, the 'King', challenges Chappell's registry of copyrights and thinks the Court should see the assignments.

Willets and his associates get convictions of 'graduated generosity'.

Dealers complain about publishers' trade practices and 'sixpenny music'.

Hawkers are included in the Leeds Conspiracy Trial, and it succeeds.

Parliament delays.

A musicseller, 'honourable' for fifty years, is caught selling piracies and explains his difficult position.

Publishers' expenses mount up.

M. P. Caldwell repeats his objections to the new bill for The Times.

The Musical Copyright Act of 1906 passes at 'the midnight hour', then receives the Royal Assent.

T. P. O'Connor is fêted.

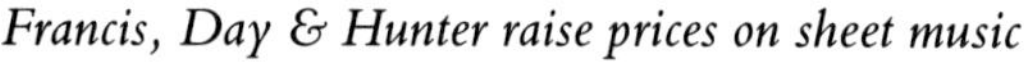

Francis, Day & Hunter raise prices on sheet music.

December 1905

The 'Great Prosecution for Conspiracy' begins.

Messrs. George Wooton, James Frederick Willetts (known as the 'Pirate King'), William Tennant, John W. Puddefoot, and William Wallace are charged in Bow Street Court with conspiracy to print, publish, and sell copies of copyrighted music without the owners' consent. The solicitor for Messrs. Chappell & Co., who are prosecuting the case, in his opening statements indicates that many other persons (engravers and printers) will be named as part of the conspiracy, some called to testify. Two classes who will not be called are the middlemen and the humbler class of life, the hawkers. He points out that in the last two and a half years, 300,000 illegal copies of Chappell's copyrights have been seized, two million belonging to other publishers. When the copyright owners became troublesome, the idea of a limited liability company of pirates was put into action. Thereafter the minute a raid was made, an action for unlawful trespass could be begun, the whole company would cease to exist, and a new one could be formed the next day to carry on the work.

In January 1904 the firm of James Fisher & Co. was registered. Willetts' name did not appear as an owner, but those of Puddefoot and Wallace, and the false names of several others, did. The purpose of the company was to publish and distribute cheap music and to give technical and legal assistance to its members who found themselves in trouble with the courts. The prosecution claims the address of the company was false, the 'whole thing a mere sham', and whatever property there was, was Willetts'.

Various witnesses offer testimony to convince the court that the case should go to trial. Evidence is given about previous cases against the defendants: 77,788 illegal copies destroyed and £10 10s. costs against John Fisher, 6 Jan. 1904; 287,792 copies destroyed and £10 10s. costs against George Wooton on 1 August 1905; in June 1903, £5 costs against W. Fisher; June 1904, £15 15s. against Willetts; 24 September 1904, £4 4s. against Tennant.

Arthur Preston testifies about the magnitude of the illegal trade with figures on the number of copies seized at different times: in June 1903, 25,000 copies at Compton Passage, Clerkenwell; October 1904, 237,000 copies at Poole Road, Hackney; January 1903, 119,000 at Boundary Lane, Walworth; and 200,000 torn copies and 11,900 complete at Ormonde Street, Holborn.[176]

An engraver who has engraved blocks for Willetts for about five years, says that some were left in various names at railway station cloak rooms and the tickets forwarded to Willetts.

'The prisoners were remanded on bail'. *MO&MTR*, p. 224

176. *Preston was an agent hired by the MPA to travel about and haul pirates into court. In the Music Division of the British Library, pressmark M. 55, is a small 4-by-7-inch notebook whose title page reads: 'Press Cuttings, Police Court Proceedings, Decisions, etc.' It is filled with loose, folded newspaper clippings along with some pasted down. The papers represented are large and small from all over Britain, and most clippings mention Preston by name.*

To help Preston in his prosecutions, about 250 lithographed piracies were bound into four, large folio volumes, and these are now in the British Library, pressmark H. 1848. a.–d, under the title, 'Pirated Music'. They contain most of the titles mentioned in the course of this chronicle, e.g.:

Crouch's Kathleen Mavourneen
de Koven's Oh, Promise Me
Lauder's She is ma Daisy
Mascheroni's Eternal City *and* For All Eternity
Piccolomini's The Toilers *and* Whisper and I shall hear
Pinsuti's Queen of the Earth
Riego's O dry those Tears
Smallwood's Fairy Barque
Sousa's El Capitan *(and seven others!)*
Sullivan's The lost Chord
Van Alstyne's In the Shade of the old apple Tree.

January 1906

The hearings in the Willetts case occupy another eight days spread over seven weeks.[177] Two hundred 'exhibits' are put in, and over fifty witnesses called—none for the defence. A sixth name is added to the conspiracy, Philip Fleming Bockenham. The case for the prosecution depends heavily on material evidence found at various premises associated with the defendants and on reports about the seizures of illegal copies.

177. *The case is also reported fully in the* L&PMTR *for 15 Nov. 1905 (pp. 27, 29) and in the* Musical News *for 6 Jan, (pp. 10–11) and 27 Jan. 1906 (pp. 78–79).*

A police constable who had been called by Mr. Preston to a van off City Road on 25 September identifies Willetts as in charge of the van. At the time, Willetts refused to give his name and walked away. The van contained over 12,000 illegal copies, including 3,000 of *Bird in a Gilded Cage*.

On 6 December 1904, at Worship Street Police Court, the destruction of 32,000 copies of pirated music was ordered and 6 guineas in costs ordered against Tennant.

A tailor, who 'did a bit' in cheap music with Fisher & Co. says he paid half-a-crown per 100 copies for the music, the company the carriage. He tells of a visit from Willetts who showed him samples from the 'People's Music Publishing Company'.

An engraver says Willetts was introduced to him as 'Mr. Chalk', and that he made blocks for him, receiving copies of the music from 'Mr. Chalk' at street corners or at public houses, leaving the finished blocks at cloak rooms at Holborn Viaduct and at Ludgate Hill stations. His commissions amounted to several pounds but he cannot be exact. His firm had made hundreds of blocks for Willetts including *The Holy City*, *Florence*, and *Spring Chicken*.

Another printer says he had worked for Puddefoot, printing for him, in two different locations, about 22,000 copies, including *Ora Pro Nobis*.

The solicitor for the defendants insists repeatedly that the publishers should be made to bring in their assignments [receipts signed by composers for certain amounts in return for the rights to a piece] in order to verify their ownership of some of the pieces in question, but the magistrate is just as adamant that the certificates of registration at Stationers' Hall are sufficient proof.

An agent for both the Musical Copyright Association and for Francis, Day & Hunter testifies about raids in which he has participated. On 14 December 1903, 45,000 illegal copies were seized in Mount Pleasant Grove, Islington, a place frequented by Willetts and Tennant. On 24 December 1903, another 73,000 copies were seized in Link St. Homerton. Willetts and Tennant were there at the time, along with men known as 'The Rabbit', 'Long Tom', and 'Robbie'. Raids on premises in Red Lion Yard, Wardour Street and at Puddefoot's place in Turnagain Lane netted 11,000 copies. In a raid in Danbury Street, Islington, over 100,000 copies were seized, and Tennant was there at the time. On 16 February 1905, about 314,000 copies were taken from stables at the rear of the Angel Arms in Clapham; 'Robbie' and 'The Rabbit' were both present.

Another agent for Francis, Day & Hunter tells of a raid on premises in Banner Street, St. Luke's on 15 November 1904. About 168,000 copies were seized. While the agents were delayed obtaining admission, those within were tearing up the music, thirty sacks full of it. Later, in connection with this raid, Tennant was summoned to Worship Street Police Court. Willetts was at the court and 'took a great interest in the proceedings'.

A 'corrector of the press' who had been employed by Willetts as a stock keeper, produced many letters gathered while working in that capacity. One from Manchester addressed to the 'Pirate King', states that unless the newest music is promptly forwarded, the writer will have to 'transfer his custom to the Pirate King at Leeds, who supplied better and more up to date music and at less cost'.

After days of such testimony the prisoners all plead not guilty and reserve their defence. The same bail is allowed to each, as before.

One of the more important statements made during the hearings comes from Mr. Muir, for the prosecution, who states at one point that 'There [has] never been a *criminal* prosecution in respect of the printing of pirated music before this case was started'.[178]

MO&MTR, pp. 303–06

February 1906

The eight days of public trial at the Old Bailey have entailed an enormous expenditure of money by the prosecution and the convictions—'of graduated generosity'—are a source of some disappointment[179] Willetts, the director of the nefarious enterprise, gets nine months without hard labour; Tennant goes to jail for two months, Puddefoot for one. Ross, the printer–journalist, will pay £50 in fines, and Wooton and Bockenham come up for judgment if they again engage in piracy.

Will the trial suppress music piracy? The writer thinks so, because the charge of conspiracy casts a wide net that could ensnare 'some firms of repute who engraved blocks from which the title pages of pirated music were printed . . . No office boy of average intelligence could have failed to understand that blocks copied from existing publications were not made in the ordinary course of business'. Evidence is now available to sustain convictions in other areas and to other parties if the piracy continues.

There is consolation for the publishers. They have proved that copyright is a property just as much as a man's watch and chain, and they have proclaimed to the world their determination to consider no cost too great in fighting to protect that property.

MO&MTR, p. 378

178. *This landmark assault on piracy succeeded because the publishers took a new tack, linking two or more persons engaged in an illegal activity and charging them under the laws against conspiracy. As recounted in* The Story of Francis, Day & Hunter, told by John Abbott, *pp. 36–37 (London: the publisher, c1952): A lawyer suggested to Mr. William Boosey that proceedings might be taken under the Conspiracy Law. The preamble of that Act says that if two or more persons conspire in an illegal manner, they can be found guilty of conspiracy. 'To publish and sell pirated music by oneself, without any outside help, would only be a civil offence'. Conviction on conspiracy charges could lead to imprisonment.*

179. *See Chappell & Co.'s statement of costs, here in note 185 at June 1906.*

Dense with details, a summary of the conspiracy trial fills twenty columns in the *MO&MTR*. Included are the summation by the prosecution, the defences offered by the solicitors for each defendant (the defendants did not take the stand), and the 'Common Serjeant's' own presentation to the jury.

The prosecution reviewed the evidence implicating and linking each defendant to the unlawful acts and to each other. The criminal intent to defraud was emphasized; these acts were not separate and unrelated offences to be solved by civil action but separate parts of an over-all arrangement to prejudice and hinder the rightful owners. Some of the witnesses, the prosecution admits, 'had as much right to be in the dock as any of the accused', but the criminal procedures made it necessary to use them in this way.

The solicitor for Willetts tried again to cast doubt on the validity of Chappell's copyrights, because the court had not forced the firm to present the assignments. 'If they were good, why were they not produced?' He has a list of forty certificates of songs claimed to be copyright in January of 1903, but at that time only eight of the forty were registered at Stationers' Hall. He notes also that one witness has testified his firm did not register songs until they were successful. Willetts' main purpose, he says, was to test the validity of these copyrights.

He also raised the possibility of a mastermind of the conspiracy, a law clerk named Johnston. Witnesses testify that Johnston 'dominated the proceedings', and uncontradicted evidence shows that the idea of the limited liability company was his. Willetts' solicitor asks why he was not called to the stand by the prosecution, implying that Johnston would have embarrassed their case. The judge later terms Johnston 'unscrupulous' on the basis of evidence submitted, but no more is heard of this shadowy person.

Tennant's solicitor pictures his client as simply a servant to Willetts, not a conspirator, and claims he knew nothing about most of the operations. He admits that the prosecution has a case for civil charges but challenges the case for criminal conspiracy.

The case against the other defendants is less damaging; statements made in their defence are brief.

The magistrate's splendid presentation of the case to the jury includes a history of musical copyright, a chronology of the events and of the conspirators' activities leading up to the trial, a review and interpretation of the evidence presented at the hearings and the trial, and balanced assessments of the importance to be attached to that evidence and the witnesses' testimony. Since no evidence or testimony has been offered for the defence, the outcome is a foregone conclusion.

Mr. Willetts' solicitor pleads for mitigation because his client has a wife and eleven children.

Mr. Tennant's solicitor echoes this plea because his client has a wife and six children. *MO&MTR*, pp. 381–87

A letter from Milgrom Bros., musicsellers, alludes to the attention-getting trial over the publishers' grievances, and notes that the musicsellers have some also. 'What conscience has the music publisher with regard to the retail traders when they charge us 16d. per copy for songs that we are obliged to sell at the same price? The publishers ought to do as they would be done unto. A certain director of Chappell & Co. on being cross-examined, refused to answer what terms they give to the trade'. Milgrom wants to know why.[180] *MO&MTR*, p. 388

180. *The* Musical News *30(10 Feb. 1906): 129–30 states that it has received many letters in the same vein from many small retailers—and appears to agree with their complaints.*

March 1906

The musicsellers in the north have hardly gotten relief from the pirates before another difficulty arises, the sale of sixpenny books of music at 4½d. 'There are mysteries about the cheap music trade which old and experienced members of the trade claim they cannot explain'.

This underselling is done chiefly by cheap booksellers and newsagents. But where do they get it? The musicsellers are unhappy with the position of the sixpenny book branch of the trade, feeling that it, first, affects the shilling book branch, and the two together affect the sale of copyright music unfavourably. Unless the underselling stops, the sixpenny trade will fall entirely into the hands of the cheap booksellers and newsagents. *MO&MTR*, p. 461

Another conspiracy hearing takes place in Leeds in February. It is laid out along the lines of the recent, successful one in London and is prosecuted by the same solicitor, Mr. Muir, for Chappell & Co. It is also the first to include hawkers.[181] Much of the testimony effectively ties the three defendants and their operations together, and those to the operations of Willetts and Fisher & Co. in London, and to a man named Cassidy in Liverpool. Several witnesses are, in fact, persons who testified in the Willetts trial previously. Mr. Muir warns that those, like Cassidy, named in the correspondence of the defendants will be the subject of future conspiracy charges. Case is adjourned until 1 March. *MO&MTR*, p. 464

181. *The decision in the great Willetts case did not touch the hawkers. Chappell, despite the enormous expense it had incurred in that trial, decided to go ahead with this Leeds Prosecution (*Min. Bk., *314). See also the entry for May 1906.*

Mr. Goodman of Chappell & Co., and Mr. Day of Francis, Day & Hunter grant interviews to the *Era*.

Mr. Goodman thinks the recent Willetts conspiracy case eminently successful. It establishes that music piracy is now indictable as a criminal conspiracy, though it does not eliminate the need for amendment of the existing copyright to provide summary protection. Mr. Caldwell, he says, can no longer 'stand up in the face of that eminent pronouncement' of the magistrate and argue that copyright is only a privilege. The prosecution required six months of preparation and 'we really cannot afford to go on with such expensive proceedings'.

He admits that Chappell & Co., and other music publishers, are involved in the election fight of Mr. Caldwell.[182]

182. *In a chapter on 'Musical Piracies' in his* Fifty Years of Music *(London: Benn Ltd. [1931]), William Boosey says 'At one election in Glasgow we ran a Socialist candidate against him' to secure the seat for the Conservative. 'We were not successful, however'. (p. 113).*

Mr. Day finds most important the great public attention focussed on the Willetts trial which, he hopes, will influence the forthcoming parliament to pass proper legislation. He conjectures that the lenient sentences were handed down because the Willetts trial was the first under the charge of criminal conspiracy to print, publish, and sell copyrighted music without consent of the owners. The Common Serjeant, however, warned that future offences would be more harshly dealt with. He regrets that in the provinces the publishers get little support; 'In Leeds the authorities have shown no sympathy whatever towards the owners of copyright'.

MO&MTR, p. 466

April 1906

Closing his letter with 'Profit nil', a musicseller 'cannot help being astonished at the indifference of publishers to their own and to their customers' interests'. Enclosing an advertisement placed in a paper by a Bolton price-cutter, he wonders why 'publishers continue to supply such persistent "cutters" . . . Even patent medicine manufacturers bind their customers not to sell below a certain price'.

MO&MTR, p. 539

A traveller wishes that his colleagues would be less reluctant to take an active hand in the fight against pirates. They should help him clear the streets of hawkers. He finds the police cooperative and urges others to follow his example. *ibid.*

The hearing in Leeds resumes on 11 March. Testimony reveals that access to the pirate's house was gained through a ruse perpetrated by a young man named Young in the employ of Alexander Wishert, agent for the Music Publishers' Association. He posed as a pirate to gain access to the house, then opened the door to the police. He had been a pirate in Liverpool, had been raided by Mr. Wishert whom he had assaulted, and for which he spent a month in jail. Now he works for Wishert, and was thought by the pirates to be one of them.

The hearing resumes again on 6 March with ten defendants on the charge sheet but only three in court—and two of these having been arrested again between the earlier hearing and this, again for selling illegal copies.

They are ordered to trial at the Leeds Assizes.

MO&MTR, pp. 539–40

A writer in *Gil blas* (Paris) says that the pirates deserve no sympathy but they have revealed a market for music among a portion of the people 'who are below what is called the public', and that publishers should exploit that market by engaging the hawkers who used to work for the pirates. *MO&MTR*, p. 540

May 1906

The case of conspiracy with intent to defraud Messrs. Chappell & Co. is tried in Leeds Crown Court on 30 March. Fifteen indictments are lodged against twelve defendants, the cases tried in three groups. After the jury has found the first group of three guilty, all of the others plead the same.

That first group consists of two hawkers, Watson and Sheridan, and a John Owen Smith, the 'Leeds Pirate King' who, it is proved, has done business on a large scale with the 'London Pirate King', Willetts, as well as other producers of illegal reprints. A witness who was the secretary to Willetts' People's Music Publishing Co. in London states that it was a perfectly legitimate business, but that Willetts' other firm, Fisher & Co.—with which Smith had done business—was engaged in piracy.

In the raid on Smith's house previous to the trial, a number of Fisher & Co.'s circulars were discovered. These announce that the firm will prepare pirated music on customers' demands if quantities of not less than 500 are ordered.[183] 'Piracy while you wait', adds the prosecution's counsel.

In summing up, His Lordship says that though it is unlawful but not criminal to sell pirated music, to combine to do that which is unlawful is itself criminal. The group is found guilty, a decision important because it establishes for the first time that hawkers as well as printers and distributors, can be held liable to imprisonment for conspiracy.

The remaining defendants enter pleas of guilty and they are sentenced—Smith to two months, two others to one month, a 'middleman' like Smith to six weeks. Eight others, all hawkers, are bound over and fined £5 each. *MO&MTR*, p. 616

183. *No copies of this document found (see 'Missing Documents', Appendix, pp. 143–4).*

Mr. George Adcock, a musicseller in Loughborough is summoned to Petty Sessions for having pirated music in his shop. Arthur

Preston, agent for the Music Publishers' Association (who was part of the prosecution in the Leeds case), had seized some sixty-six copies from Adcock's shop.

The defendant tends to his own aggressive defence. He is outraged at being treated as a common pirate after fifty years of honourable dealing. He asks Mr. Preston why the Association has not investigated conditions in Loughborough sooner; the pirates have been selling openly on the streets for years, and the Association has done nothing. The 'germ' of piracy is the high price of music, he says, and though he stocks thousands of copies of copyright music, he also buys from the pirates—not for profit, but because his customers ask for cheap music. If he does not or can not supply them, they simply walk down to the market or find a hawker in the street near his shop.

The Bench orders the music handed over to the copyright owner and fines Adcock costs. *MO&MTR*, pp. 617–18

The *Daily Telegraph* thinks the recent court cases 'have put an entirely new complexion' on musical piracy but that complete abolition is a long way off unless the government does its duty and brings in a bill to protect copyright owners. 'It has been left to a private firm to establish that those responsible for systematic piracy of music are engaged in criminal traffic'. *MO&MTR*, p. 618

'Argus' reports that dealers in northern England are in a much lighter mood since the successful prosecution of pirates and the agents. 'One has no longer the choice of a score of pirated editions at twopence each in any central thoroughfare or market, as was the case a few months ago'. Business in copyright songs in the shops has picked up. *MO&MTR*, p. 619

Under the caption 'Poor Prospect of Government Copyright Act this Season', the *MO&MTR* summarizes an article in *Truth* reproving Parliament for its delay. As no substantial change in the law is necessary—only the provision of means to enforce it—it is difficult to understand why legislation is slow. Nor is there any need for more discussion of the criminal nature of piracy; two expensive prosecutions have established that. *MO&MTR*, p. 621

June 1906

Mr. Walter Slaughter, claiming to have suffered greatly from the pirates, has decided to seize 'music of mine hawked by street men on sight'. He has already done so, capturing two dozen copies in

Upper Street, Islington, last week. He considers anyone who buys a pirated song a receiver of stolen goods. 'Over three thousand men in London get a dishonest living by selling pirated music', and he says everyone should support Mr. T. P. O'Connor's new bill.[184]

MO&MTR, p. 698

Music publishers are rallying around Messrs. Chappell & Co. which has borne the major expenses in the recent prosecutions. Large debts for court costs remain outstanding and the *MO&MTR* suggests subscriptions to a fund to assist the firm.[185]

MO&MTR, p. 701

July 1906

The text of Mr. O'Connor's Musical Copyright Bill, three short clauses, is reprinted verbatim by the *MO&MTR* which notes that its progress in Parliament is being blocked: 'Every night at eleven o'clock an objection is raised in the stereotyped form [i.e., the public's need for cheap music]. The two members most conspicuous in their opposition are Mr. Harwood and Mr. Byles . . .'.[186]

From *The Times* the *MO&MTR* reprints a long letter from Mr. James Caldwell describing the bill, its history, and—to his mind—its many faults. Clause I, he says, does not deal with the real pirate, the printer, the real trafficker, who can already be dealt with successfully in criminal conspiracy cases. It changes piracy from a civil to a criminal case placing the 'onus of proof on the accused', unlike earlier bills. It requires a penalty of imprisonment, placing it first in order, with fines, not exceeding five pounds, as the alternative. Under Clause I any constable may take into custody, without warrant, 'any person who sells, exposes, offers or has in his possession for sale any pirated music'. The power is without restriction. At the instance of an owner or publisher any 'rival in trade' may be 'marched off in custody through the public street'. Earlier bills placed limitations on the power of apprehension.

Clause II attempts to set up practical search warrants that will not come under the usual conditions of search warrants, namely as they appear in the Merchandise Marks Act. Mr. O'Connor's bill not only overturns the provisions of the bill of last session and the bill of 1904 as amended, but it is remarkable for what it omits. There is no appeal to quarter sessions where the value of the article is over 40s. Not carried over from the amended bill of 1904 are the following:

a) the clause of limitation, stating that no offence committed prior to registration is actionable (a provision recommended by the Royal Commission on Copyright in 1878);

b) the clause of registration of copyright, requiring the owner to print on the title page the date of first publication;

184. *In the minutes of the Annual General meeting of the MPA for 22 June 1906, it is reported that the MPA's agents seized 984,314 illegal copies and started proceedings in connection with 122 seizures. In most of those cases, costs were recovered or the defendants remanded to prison. In addition, there were many prosecutions 'by voluntary agents working under our instructions . . .'.*

185. *A year later, 'in response to the musical profession and the music trade', Chappell & Co., in a letter to the* Musical Times *for 1 Feb. 1907 (p. 111) submit an accounting of some of the costs:*

the Willetts prosecution — *3,000 guineas*
the Leeds prosecution — *1,000 guineas*
Parliamentary expenses — *£2,500*

Total £6,700

Towards these expenses, they have received by subscription:

from music publishers and the trade — *£1,363*
from composers published by Chappell — *£537*
from composers published by other houses — *£185*

The editor points out that the expenses shown are far from the total cost borne by Chappell and by many others.

Twenty years later, an article, 'Those Music Pirates', in the MO&MTR *for September 1926 (p. 1243) comments on Chappell's expenses, raising these figures: 'Chappell alone had spent between £8000 and £9000 in suppressing the wrong and in promotion of the Musical Copyright Act. The actual cost incurred in the successful prosecution of Willets, the master mind of the whole conspiracy, was three thousand guineas, whilst a Leeds prosecution cost a thousand guineas more'.*

186. *Mr. O'Connor and the bill's other supporters struggled throughout the session to have the bill recognized as a government measure, not a private bill, for until a bill became a*

government measure, only one dissenting voice could 'put it on the shelf'. MO&MTR, *Nov. 1906.*

c) the clause of registration by owner, requiring the owner to register the copyright within one month of the date of publication, setting forth the true name and place of abode of the owner; and

d) the clause of assignments of copyright, whereby every assignee within one month will enter the copyright in the register setting forth his true name and address and the deed of assignment.

If these protections were considered necessary in 1878, when only civil action was permitted, they are imperative now that criminal prosecution can take place under the summary jurisdiction acts.

Caldwell cautions that great care must be taken in granting any exceptional legislation for it is apt to be claimed as a precedent later.

MO&MTR, pp. 775–76

The *MO&MTR* reprints an article which it calls 'What *The Times* Thinks' about the new copyright bill. It summarizes the piracy problem and the history of legislative actions against it, expressing the hope that the new bill will go through without attempts 'to mix up a simple question of morality with irrelevant talk about cheap music and "rings" of publishers'. *MO&MTR*, p. 776

August 1906

In a conversation with the *Westminster Gazette* Mr. T. P. O'Connor gives many of the reasons for passing the bill he has introduced. He also answers, though not specifically, some of the questions which have been raised about its provisions.

He recounts a number of personal tragedies that have resulted from the growth of piracy. George Le Brunn, perhaps a few years previously the most popular song writer in England, whose income was thousands of pounds a year, made only four pounds from his songs in 1905. Signor Mascheroni, his income diminished because of the piracies, was forced to return to Italy, almost penniless. Women as well as men are hurt. Terese del Riego's *O dry those Tears* has been sold by the pirates in hundreds of thousands of copies. Another, Guy d'Hardelot, has had her famous song, *Because*, pirated repeatedly. M. Messager, the composer of *Veronique*, came to London to supervise its production and found songs from it being hawked outside the theatre. In France, an English composer in such a situation could have the hawker promptly arrested.

O'Connor goes on to review how piracy grew to such proportions, to explain why the existing legislation is incapable of eliminating it, and to justify the provisions of his bill.

MO&MTR, pp. 848–49

'Mercury', in 'Trade Memoranda', notes that the copyright bill is just about to be enacted, having passed its third reading. Composers, publishers, and retailers 'can enter upon the ensuing autumn season with a feeling that their respective brains, plates and copies can be fairly called their own'.

Ground lost the last few years will never be regained. The extreme indifference of the public at large is also painfully apparent. But all can be thankful and grateful to Mr. O'Connor for his untiring exertions, and to the Prime Minister, the Home Secretary, and the Attorney General for their continuing support. Mercury suggests a testimonial for them before Christmas.

The bill may have weaknesses in practice; time will tell. Some of its provisions offer wide discretionary powers that must be carefully exercised, without indiscriminate zeal, to punish the criminal misdemeanant but not to harrass those who err through ignorance. Otherwise, public indifference may turn to public indignation.

MO&MTR, pp. 849–50

A PIRATE CRAFT!

T. P. O'Connor (Captain of War Sloop in Chase). "The Rogues! This ought to sink 'em!"

Reprinted by Special Permission of the Proprietors of *Punch*.

MO&MTR, p. 849

'Success in Sight!' says the *MO&MTR*. After a stormy voyage, the bill, as of 26 July, is in sight of port.

To illustrate the sort of stormy weather the bill has weathered, some of the points raised for and against the bill in committee are printed. Most have been discussed before, repeatedly, over the past few years. The transcript shows clearly why the publishers are indebted to Mr. O'Connor and to the Attorney General; the latter's responses to amendments and other parliamentary devices designed to cripple the bill were masterful. One by one all attempts to weaken the legislation by such means were voted down.

MO&MTR, p. 853

4 August 1906

The bill, so long fought-over, so long-awaited, becomes an Act, effective this date.[187] It is two pages long:

187. *According to Carlene Mair in* The Chappell Story, 1811–1961 *(London: Chappell & Co., Ltd., 1961), pp. 34–35, the Act finally passed 'in a highly dramatic manner; [it] was squeezed through Parliament in the very last minutes of the last night of the session'.*

CHAPTER 36.

An Act to amend the law relating to Musical Copyright.

[4th August 1906.]

BE it enacted by the King's most Excellent Majesty, by and with the advice and consent of the Lords Spiritual and Temporal, and Commons, in this present Parliament assembled, and by the authority of the same, as follows:

Penalty for being in possession of pirated music.

1.—(1) Every person who prints, reproduces, or sells, or exposes, offers, or has in his possession for sale, any pirated copies of any musical work, or has in his possession any plates for the purpose of printing or reproducing pirated copies of any musical work, shall (unless he proves that he acted innocently) be guilty of an offence punishable on summary conviction, and shall be liable to a fine not exceeding five pounds, and on a second or subsequent conviction to imprisonment with or without hard labour for a term not exceeding two months or to a fine not exceeding ten pounds: Provided that a person convicted of an offence under this Act who has not previously been convicted of such an offence, and who proves that the copies of the musical work in respect of which the offence was committed had printed on the title page thereof a name and address purporting to be that of the printer or publisher, shall not be liable to any penalty under this Act unless it is proved that the copies were to his knowledge pirated copies.

(2) Any constable may take into custody without warrant any person who in any street or public place sells or exposes, offers, or has in his possession for sale any pirated copies of any such musical work as may be specified in any general written authority addressed to the chief officer of police, and signed by the apparent owner of the copyright in such work or his agent thereto authorised in writing, requesting the arrest, at the risk of such owner, of all persons found committing offences under this section in respect to such work, or who offers for sale any pirated copies of any such specified musical work by personal canvass or by personally delivering advertisements or circulars.

(3) A copy of every written authority addressed to a chief officer of police under this section shall be open to inspection at all reasonable hours by any person without payment of any fee, and any person may take copies of or make extracts from any such authority.

(4) Any person aggrieved by a summary conviction under this section may in England or Ireland appeal to a court of quarter sessions, and in Scotland under and in terms of the Summary Prosecutions Appeals (Scotland) Act, 1875. 38 & 39 Vict. c. 62.

Right of entry by police for execution of Act.

2.—(1) If a court of summary jurisdiction is satisfied by information on oath that there is reasonable ground for suspecting that an offence against this Act is being committed on any premises, the court may grant a search warrant authorising the constable named therein to enter the premises between the hours of six of the clock in the morning and nine of the clock in the evening, and, if necessary, to use force for making such entry, whether by breaking open doors or otherwise, and to seize any copies of any musical work or any plates in respect of which he has reasonable ground for suspecting that an offence against this Act is being committed.

(2) All copies of any musical work and plates seized under this section shall be brought before a court of summary jurisdiction, and if proved to be pirated copies or plates intended to be used for the printing or reproduction of pirated copies shall be forfeited and destroyed or otherwise dealt with as the court think fit.

Definitions.

3. In this Act—

The expression "pirated copies" means any copies of any musical work written, printed, or otherwise reproduced without the consent lawfully given by the owner of the copyright in such musical work:

The expression "musical work" means a musical work in which there is a subsisting copyright, and which has been registered in accordance with the provisions of the Copyright Act, 1842, or of the International Copyright Act, 1844, which registration may be effected notwithstanding anything in the International Copyright Act, 1886:

5 & 6 Vict. c. 45.
7 & 8 Vict. c. 12.
49 & 50 Vict. c. 33.

The expression "plates" includes any stereotype or other plates, stones, matrices, transfers, or negatives used or intended to be used for printing or reproducing copies of any musical work: Provided that the expressions "pirated copies" and "plates" shall not, for the purposes of this Act, be deemed to include perforated music rolls used for playing mechanical instruments, or records used for the reproduction of sound waves, or the matrices or other appliances by which such rolls or records respectively are made:

The expression "chief officer of police"—

(*a*) with respect to the City of London, means the Commissioner of City Police;

(*b*) elsewhere in England has the same meaning as in the Police Act, 1890; 53 & 54 Vict. c. 45.

(*c*) in Scotland has the same meaning as in the Police (Scotland) Act, 1890; 53 & 54 Vict. c. 67.

(*d*) in the police district of Dublin metropolis means either of the Commissioners of Police for the said district;

(*e*) elsewhere in Ireland means the District Inspector of the Royal Irish Constabulary:

The expression "court of summary jurisdiction" in Scotland means the sheriff or any magistrate of any royal, parliamentary, or police burgh officiating under the provisions of any local or general police Act.

Short title.

4. This Act may be cited as the Musical Copyright Act, 1906.

The bill has passed and has secured the Royal Assent.[188] 'We may perhaps be permitted to congratulate one another all round. Thanks are due to Messrs. Chappell, to the other publishers who worked hand in hand with them, and to Mr. T. P. O'Connor, for their hard and faithful work. We hope that it may now be a case of "rest and be thankful". We here warn our friends the pirates that the publishers are in earnest, that all the preliminaries are arranged and that a test case will be prosecuted at the earliest opportunity'.[189]

MO&MTR, p. 930

188. *The Act will remain in force until 1 June 1957 when it (as amended by the Copyright Act of 1911) and the Musical (Summary Proceedings) Act of 1902 are both repealed and consolidated into the Copyright Act, 1956.*

189. *None of this determination, or even more curious any elation over the passage of the new Act is to be found in minutes of the meetings of the MPA and its Committee after this date!*

December 1906

In an interview with the American *Musical Age*, Mr. O'Connor reveals some of the compromises and actions that were necessary to secure passage of the new bill. It was once killed by one member of Parliament who talked in opposition to it from three o'clock one afternoon until five o'clock the next morning.[190] When new legislation was later introduced, opposition was encountered from the Gramophone & Typewriter Co., Ltd., one of the most powerful English companies.

With Mr. Boosey's advice, it was decided to avoid G & T's resistance by inserting a clause exempting music rolls and gramophone records from copyright lawsuits ('a question, however, sure to rise again')[191] in order to 'get at the root of our present evil—the kerbstone hawkers'.

MO&MTR, pp. 223–24

190. *Some kind of bill had been introduced in just about every session of Parliament since the passage of the Copyright Act of 1902.*

191. *As indeed it did! The Copyright Act of 1911 amended that of 1906 to deal with these problems, but it was not entirely successful. A better solution was reached when the 1956 consolidation Act came into force in 1957.*

Over 200 persons attend the complimentary dinner for Mr. O'Connor on 19 November at the Hotel Cecil. The Duke of Argyll, presiding, introduces Mr. O'Connor 'amidst repeated cheers', who modestly praises others for having worked so long to prepare the way for his 'completing touch'. He recalls the 1902 bill which was introduced with good intentions but 'went upstairs' to be amended with the result tht 'the evil, which was a dwarf before the bill passed the Lords, suddenly became a giant'. In 1905 another bill was introduced and defeated by a 'blocking' motion against the second reading. With Mr. Boosey's help, however, changes were made and at last the bill was 'starred' by the Government, which helped assure its passage. As a result, 'musical piracy [has] already almost disappeared. (Cheers)'.

MO&MTR, p. 226

January 1907

'Yes, the year 1906 has gone, and the accounts of the music trade are being made up with mingled feelings ... The predominant feeling is one of thankfulness and quiet content'. A year ago, upon the eve of Christmas 1905, Willetts and his crew were committed for trial on conspiracy, and their subsequent conviction prepared the way for the new law. 'We may or may not think the present the best of all possible governments . . . but [it] must at least be credited with an act of common justice'.

[The publisher has been served; so too the composer. But what of the public?]

Ironically—only a few months after passage of the new Act—a small paragraph under 'Trade Jottings', informs readers that Messrs. Francis, Day & Hunter, music publishers, declare the necessity for selling under price "inexistent". The firm urges dealers to revise their prices to the public, to 'discontinue their self-sacrificing policy', and to make 6d. net mean 6d net. 'We intend on and after January 1st, 1907, raising our trade rates fifty per cent'!

MO&MTR, p. 311

May 1909

The music publishing business is reviving; Messrs. Chappell & Co. rebound.

Messrs. Chappell's New Premises.

THERE was a scene of life and activity the other afternoon when Messrs. Chappell invited their friends and clients to afternoon tea at their Bond Street premises. The new suite of pianoforte show rooms have been designed by Mr. Walter Crane in the style of Queen Anne, with dead white walls. Every type of pianoforte was exhibited, including concert grands and many models, down to the smallest folding instruments for yachts.

The interior of the front shop, with its spacious proportions, has been entirely reconstructed, all the old woodwork, furniture and fittings having given place to fumed oak. Polished oak parquet flooring has been adopted throughout the shop, galleries and show rooms. Green Turkey carpets are to be noted in the centre of the shop, along the front of the several counters and through the galleries. This colour scheme of oak and green makes a very attractive and restful feature of these newly modelled rooms.

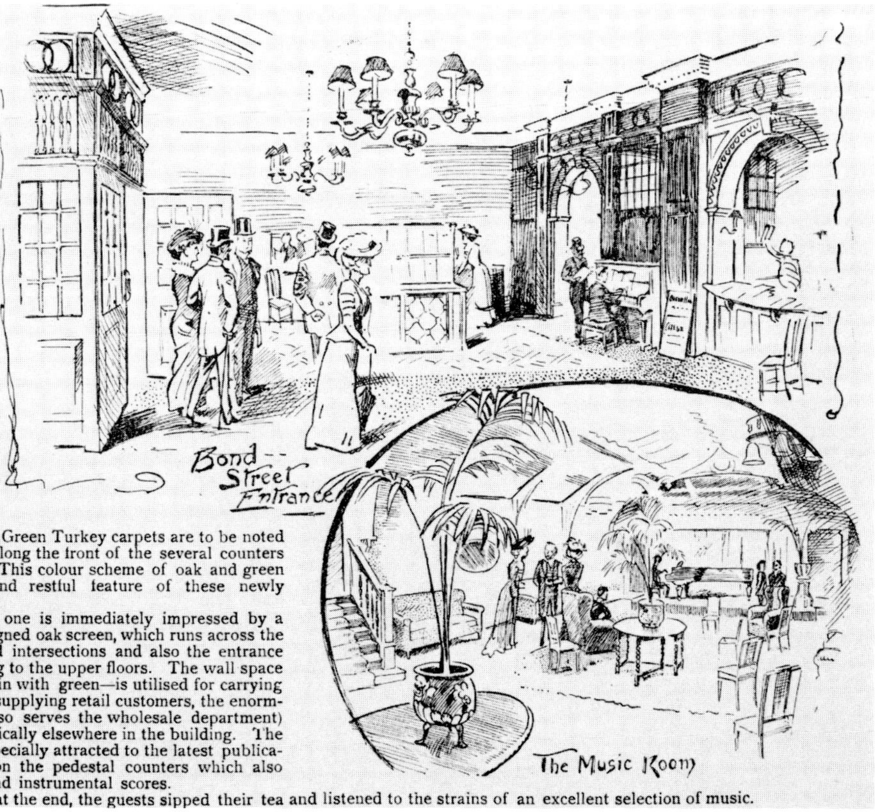

Upon entering the shop, one is immediately impressed by a massive yet artistically designed oak screen, which runs across the entire width. It has arched intersections and also the entrance to the main staircase leading to the upper floors. The wall space—with the shelves covered in with green—is utilised for carrying an assortment of music for supplying retail customers, the enormous reserve stock (which also serves the wholesale department) being stored away systematically elsewhere in the building. The attention of the visitor is specially attracted to the latest publications, arranged tastefully on the pedestal counters which also contain books and vocal and instrumental scores.

In an annexe (or lounge) at the end, the guests sipped their tea and listened to the strains of an excellent selection of music.

MO&MTR, p. 589

Epilogue

The Copyright Act of 1906 finished the pirates. Illegal copying and distribution of sheet music on a large scale was never again much of a problem. Some small operations continued (or started up), as did a few big ones, but the court cases continued, too; Arthur Preston fought on vigorously and with much success for several more years as the agent for the Music Publishers' Association.[192] For a while, the magazines and newspapers of the day reported prosecutions for piracy as excitedly as before, but the accounts became more desultory as time went by. The days of melodramatic 'raids' and captures of truckloads of 'booty' were just about over. Gradually the trade reports in both the *MO&MTR* and the *L&PMTR* forgot about the pirates, then paid less attention to music publishing interests in general and more to the trade in musical instruments. Even that began, in time, to consume less space.

192. *In May of 1909, the* MO&MTR *carried a lengthy article about the capture of some 10,000 copies of a single song being hauled in a donkey cart in Cassland Road. In the donkey's stable were later found 32,000 copies of about forty-five other songs. The* MO&MTR*'s trade correspondent, 'Mercury', on another page alleged that 'the prime mover in a gigantic undertaking is still at large . . . [Piracy] is now a carefully organized scheme. Who is at the back of it?'*

The Music Defence 'Department' of the Music Publishers' Association, formed specifically to combat the pirates, lived on for some months after passage of the Act, but in 1907, with the reorganization of the Association, it too dropped from view. The publishers remained at odds with retail musicsellers who continued to complain in letters to the journals about novelties, travellers' practices, 'net' pricing, underselling to professionals—and all the other publishers' policies that had bothered them through the years. Loopholes in the copyright law bothered some people (the retailers more, apparently, than the publishers) but the remaining problems did not strike fire or provoke sustained vehemence from any group. Little more is heard of *petits droits* and the Société des Auteurs, Compositeurs et Éditeurs de Musique.

The traditional British music hall, popularizer of so much of the material stolen by the pirates, went into decline and by the end of World War I was first threatened, then supplanted by 'the review' and American ragtime. The radio and the gramophone accorded the public new modes of entertainment. The public sales of engraved music plates and copyrights conducted by the auctioneer Puttick & Simpson in Leicester Square—which numbered over 100 from 1850 to 1900—began to decline in frequency and quality. The decline coincided with and matched that of the music hall and became more rapid after 1906.

The refractory Mr. Caldwell and his cohorts may not have been entirely wrong nor the obdurate publishers entirely in the right in these heated years. While the ethical aspects of the battle between them are quite clear—piracy *is* immoral and it *is* dishonest to cheat a composer of the fruits of his creative mind and gifted ear—the publishers were not totally virtuous. The pirates and their apologizers, Caldwell and the rest, were correct when they stated that the cheap reprints were helping to satisfy the needs of a great mass of people who could not afford legitimate prints—whose prices, many times, the publishers kept artificially high. That was not, of course, why the pirates engaged in their shady business, but there is a grain of truth in their excuse. Additionally, despite the enormous inroads they made on the publishers' profits—and the even more grievous harm done some composers—the scoundrels also helped to popularize and whet the public's appetite for the specific pieces stolen and whole *genre* represented. Perhaps, as Caldwell and those on his side insisted all along, the widespread availability of that cheap music even may have improved the public's taste.

All of that notwithstanding, piracy was wrong, and the Copyright Act of 1906 was desperately needed to stop it.

Its importance can hardly be overestimated; it was discussed and its effects analyzed in the *MO&MTR* and other periodicals and newspapers for a number of years. Curiously, within what now seems to be a short time, occasional articles began to recapitulate the history of the war with the pirates—as though most of the readers had not lived through it!

Piracy on a monstrous scale disappeared. The problems of copyright did not, but those connected with performing rights came to the fore with the advent of the gramophone and radio broadcasting. These were later exacerbated by the growth of the jukebox, the movie and sound recording industries. Today, it is TV and videotaping over which another war—new, yet not new—is being fought. Copyright and performing rights grow ever more complex, and legislative bodies remain as slow to act as they were at the turn of the century. As if those seemingly immortal difficulties were not enough, illegal copying has also revived. It may not be as organized and flagrantly felonious as it was in 1900, but for the publisher of today, the compact home and office copier holds equivalent terrors, evokes similar rages, and fuels the same litigious zeal as did the Pirate King, his henchmen and counterparts, and their scruffy products nearly a hundred years ago—back in the 'good old days'.

APPENDIX

'Missing Documents'

1884
A LETTER ... to Sir Charles Tupper, High Commissioner for Canada, from the Music Publishers' Association Sub-Committee, dated 23 Dec. 1884. It was subsequently printed in over 500 copies and sent to newspaper editors throughout Canada.

1884
A POSTER ... offering £10 reward to anyone offering information leading to the conviction of persons bringing American piracies into England through the seaports. 150 copies were sent to Newcastle, 300 to Glasgow, 50 to Hull, others to Liverpool, etc.

1888
A NOTICE ... issued by the Music Publishers' Association about 'Music Copying' which was reprinted in several magazines (as here). It was later printed on a single card along with the notice about the 'Song Folio' (1890; below) and widely distributed.

MUSIC COPYING.

Notice is hereby given that by virtue of the 5 & 6 Vict., cap. 45, sec. 2, the sole and exclusive liberty of making manuscript or other copies of copyright works is vested in the owner of such copyright, and any other persons making such copies without the permission of the said owner render themselves liable to heavy penalities or damages.

The transposition of copyright songs into other keys is an unlawful copying. By order,

G. DIXEY,
Secretary Music Publishers' Association.
9, Air Street, Regent Street, W., Jan. 1888.

1890
A NOTICE ... issued by the Music Publishers' Association about the 'Song Folio', reprinted in magazines (as below) and on a single card with the above notice about 'Music Copying'.

"Notice is hereby given, that by virtue of 5 & 6 Vict., cap. 45, sec. 23, any person having in his possession 'The Song Folio,' or any other book containing copyright music unlawfully printed or imported without the written consent of the proprietor of the copyright therein, is liable to action at law to compel the delivery up of such book and the payment of damages to the proprietor of the copyright."

1902
AN AUTHORITY ... as a result of the passage of the Copyright Act of 1902, issued by many music publishers and sent to hundreds of musicsellers throughout the country. It was reprinted in a number of magazines and newspapers, as follows:

To
of
In pursuance of The Musical (Summary Proceedings) Copyright Act, 1902, Section 2, We, the undersigned,
Music Publishers, being the apparent owners of each of the under-mentioned Musical Works, and of the Copyright therein namely : –
[here follows the list of works]
do hereby as from the 1st day of October, 1902, appoint you our Agent and do hereby authorize you to, at our own risk, request in writing on enclosed blue forms, any Constable to, without Warrant, seize from any person or persons all pirated copies of the said Works or either of them which may be hawked, carried about, sold, or offered for sale by such person or persons.

Signed............................

1902
A NOTICE ... to accompany the AUTHORITY (above), was furnished in quantities to the musicsellers, to be served on constables. It was also reprinted in a number of magazines and newspapers, as here:

To

Constable No.

In pursuance of The Musical (Summary Proceedings) Copyright Act, 1902, Section 2, I of in the (County, City, or Borough) of being the Agent thereto authorized in writing by the apparent owners of the under-mentioned Musical Works and of the Copyright therein, namely :—

Alice, where art Thou ?
Because I love You
Better Land, The
Bird in the Gilded Cage, The
Brooklyn Cake Walk
By the Fountain
Crossing the Bar
Daddy
Down South Barn Dance
Dream of Paradise, A
Good-bye, Mignonette
Heavenly Song, A
Holy City, The
Honeysuckle and the Bee
I may be Crazy
Juliana
Killarney
Lost Chord, The
Ma Rainbow Coon
Maud, Maud, Maud (Toreador).
Mona
O Dry those Tears
Oh Flo (the Motor Car Song)
Ora Pro Nobis
El Capitan March (P. Sousa)
Everybody's loved by someone
Flight of Ages, The
For all Eternity
Frangesa March
Garden of Sleep, The
Gates of the West
Gift, The
Good-bye, Dolly Gray
Pliny, Come kiss yo' Baby !
Promise of Life, The
Queen of the Earth
Shade of the Palm, The
Six little Wives (San Toy)
Skylark, Skylark
Smoke, Smoke, Smoke
Star of Bethlehem, The
Star of my Soul
Stars and Stripes for ever March
Sunflower and the Sun
Tell Me, Pretty Maiden
Whisper and I shall Hear

request you to, without warrant, seize from the person whom I now show you the pirated copies of any of the said Musical Works he is now hawking or carrying about.

Signed..... ....

1902

A 'CAUTION' ... issued by the London Metropolitan Police about 1 October 1902, warned hawkers and pedlars about the force of the Musical Copyright Act of 1902. It was reprinted in various magazines and newspapers:

"The attention of hawkers, pedlars, and others is directed to the Musical (Summary Proceedings) Copyright Act, 1902 (2 Edward VII., chapter 15), which provides as follows :—

"'If any person shall hawk, carry about, sell, or offer for sale any pirated copy of any musical work, every such pirated copy may be seized by any constable without warrant, on the request in writing of the apparent owner of the copyright in such work, or of his agent thereto authorized in writing, and at the risk of such owner.

"'On seizure of any such copies, they shall be conveyed by such constable before a Court of Summary Jurisdiction, and, on proof that they are infringements of copyright, shall be forfeited or destroyed, or otherwise dealt with as the Court may think fit.

"'"Musical work" means any combination of melody and harmony, or either of them, printed, reduced to writing, or otherwise graphically produced or reproduced.

"'"Pirated musical work" means any musical work written, printed, or otherwise reproduced, without the consent lawfully given by the owner of the copyright in such musical work.'

"Instructions have been given to the constables of the Metropolitan Police to enforce the provisions of the above-mentioned Act, which comes into operation on the 1st day of October, 1902.

"A. C. Bruce,

"The Acting Commissioner of Police of the Metropolis."

1903–05

CATALOGUES ... issued by the pirates. One is known to have been distributed in London in March 1903, another in Leeds in August 1905. There may have been others.

1904

A PRINTED FORM ... which music publishers reported they were sending to composers, stated that they would no longer publish any music until Parliament did something to protect musical properties. Chappell was one of the first to send out the notice. The statement was reprinted and paraphrased in a number of magazines and newspapers of the time.

1905

A DECLARATION ... signed by thirty-seven music publishers at meetings on 7 and 15 April 1905 stated that publishers would no longer issue new works, no new contracts for royalties would be written, and no advertising would be placed until Parliament moved to stop the piracies.

1905

AN 'OFFICIAL' DOCUMENT ... from the pirates announced the formation of a limited company in February 1905. It was widely circulated.

1905

A 'MANIFESTO' ... decrying the Copyright Bill then before Parliament was issued in the thousands by James Caldwell, M.P. from Glasgow.

Bibliography

Abbott, John. *The Story of Francis, Day & Hunter*. London: Francis, Day & Hunter, 1952.
Chapter Four, 'Pirates', pp. 29–39; Chapter Eleven, 'The Copyright Act of 1911', pp. 67–71.

Altick, Richard D. *The English Common Reader; a Social History of the Mass Reading Public, 1800–1900*. Chicago: Univ. of Chicago Press [c1957].

———. *Victorian People and Ideas*. New York: Norton [1973].

Annual Bibliography of Victorian Studies, ed. by Brahma Chaudhuri, 1977– . Edmonton, Alberta: Litir Database [c1980–].

Balfour, Arthur James. *Economic Notes on Insular Free Trade*. London: Longmans, Green & Co., 1903

Barnes, J. J. *Free Trade in Books: a Study of the London Book Trade since 1800*. Oxford: Clarendon Press, 1964.

Birrell, Augustine. *In the Name of the Bodleian and other Essays*. London: Eliot Stock, 1905. (Includes 'A few Words about Copyright in Books').

———. *Seven Lectures on the Law and History of Copyright in Books*. London: Cassell, 1899.

Blagden, Cyprian. *The Stationers' Company; a History, 1403–1959*. Stanford, California: Stanford Univ. Press, 1977, c1960.

Book Selling and Book Buying: Aspects of the Nineteenth-Century British and North American Book Trade, ed. by Richard G. Landon. London and Chicago: American Library Association [c1978].

Boosey, Thomas and Z. T. Purday. *Assumed Copyright in Foreign Authors. Judgement of the Case in Boosey v. Purday ... June 5, 1849*. London: F. Elsworth [1843!]

Boosey, William. *Fifty Years of Music*. London: Ernest Benn, Ltd. [1931].

Crowest, Frederick James. *Phases of Musical England*. London: Remington and Co., 1881.

Cutler, Edward. *The Law of Musical and Dramatic Copyright*. Rev. ed. London: Cassell, 1892.

———. *A Manual of Musical Copyright Law. For the Use of Music-publishers and Artists*. London: Simpkin, Marshall [etc.], 1905.

Goodman, Andrew. *Gilbert and Sullivan at Law*. Rutherford, N. J.: Fairleigh Dickinson Univ. Press [1983].

Great Britain. Home Dept. Musical Copyright Committee. *Report of the Departmental Committee appointed ... to inqure into the Piracy of Musical Publications, with Evidence and Appendix*. London: H.M.S.O., 1904. (*Parliamentary Papers*, v. 79, pp. 227–381).

Halsbury's Laws of England. 4th ed. London: Butterworth, 1973– .
See especially vol. 9, 'Contempt of Corporations', pp. 509–22, 525–32, 536–37.

Hurd, Michael. *Vincent Novello and Company*. London: Granada [1981].

Isaacs, Sidney Charles. *The Law Relating to Theatres, Music-halls ... including the Law of Musical and Dramatic Copyrights*. London: Stevens & Sons, 1927.

Judge, Cyril Bathurst. *Elizabethan Book Pirates*. Cambridge, Mass.: Harvard Univ. Press, 1934.

Krummel, Donald W. 'Music Publishing', Chapter 3, pp. 46–59 in *Music in Britain; the Romantic Age, 1800–1914*, ed. by Nicholas Temperley. London: Athlone Press [1981].

London. Federation of British Music Industries. *The Directory of the British Music Trade Industries*. London, 1925– .

London & Provincial Music Trades Review. v. 1–38. London: G. D. Ernest & Co., 1877/78–1915.

For successor, see *Music Trades Review*, 1916– .

The Lute; a Monthly Journal of Music News. v. 1–17. London, 1883–1899.

Magazine of Music and Journal of the Musical Reform Association, v. 1–14. London, 1884–1897.

Mair, Carlene. *The Chappell Story, 1811–1961.* London: Chappell & Co., Ltd., 1961.

Middleton, Richard. 'Popular Music of the Lower Classes', pp. 63–91 in *Music in Britain; the Romantic Age, 1800–1914*, ed. by Nicholas Temperley. London: Athlone Press [1981].

Monthly Musical Record. London: Augener & Co., 1871– .

Music and Letters. Oxford: Oxford Univ. Press, 1920– .

Music Publishers' Association. *Minute Book* [a scrapbook, ca. 10″ thick, partly unpaged, containing ms. and printed minutes and reports of the Association's and its Committee's meeting, 1881– . At the Office of the Association, Kingsway, London.]

Musical Directory, Annual & Almanack. London: Rudall, Carte, & Co., 1853–1931.

Musical Herald [formerly *The Tonic Sol-fa Reporter*]. London: J. Curwen (& Son), 1853–1920.

The Musical News; a Weekly Journal of Music. London: Office of the 'Musical News' Syndicate, 1891–1929.

Musical Opinion and Music Trade Review. London, 1877/78– .

Musical Standard. London, 1862–1871.

———. *New Series.* London: Reeves & Turner, 1871–1893.

———. *Illustrated Series.* London, 1894–1912.

Musical Times. London: Novello, 1844– .

Myers, Robin. *The British Book Trade from Caxton to the Present Day.* London: Andre Deutsch [1973].

Nettel, Reginald. 'The Influence of the Industrial Revolution on English Music', pp. 23–40. *Proceedings of the Royal Musical Association* 72 (1945–46).

New Cambridge Bibliography of English Literature, George Watson, General ed. Cambridge: Univ. Press, 1969–77.
Copyright, 19th Century, vol. 3, pp. 71–76.

Nowell-Smith, Simon. *International Copyright Law and the Publisher in the Reign of Queen Victoria.* Oxford: Clarendon Press, 1968.

Parkinson, John. 'Pirates and Publishers', *Performing Right* 58 (Dec. 1972): 20–22.

Patterson, Lyman Roy. *Copyright in Historical Perspective.* Nashville, Tenn.: Vanderbilt Univ. Press, 1968.

Pearsall, Ronald. *Edwardian Popular Music.* Newton Abbott: David & Charles [c1975].

———. *Victorian Popular Music.* Detroit: Gale Research [c1973].

Plant, Marjorie. *The English Book Trade: an Economic History of the Making and Selling of Books.* London: George Allen & Unwin, Ltd. [1965].

Poole, H. Edmund and Donald W. Krummel. 'Printing and Publishing of Music,' *The New Grove Dictionary of Music and Musicians*, 20 vols., ed. Stanley Sadie. London: Macmillan, 1980, XV, 232–74.

Preston, George Arthur. *Clipping Book.* [Newspaper cuttings relating to pirated music. On title page in ms.: 'Press cuttings. Police Court Proceedings, Decisions, etc.' Compiled by Preston, most clippings mention him, but not all. Many note newspaper source and date; many do not.]

———. *Pirated Music* [a collection of ca. 250 song sheets, lithographed by pirates. In 4 bound vols. Probably carried with Preston as he travelled to prosecute pirates and hawkers.]

Provincial Music Traders' Association. *Directory.* Windsor: T. E. Luff, 1889– .

Reeves, William. *Reeves Musical Directory, with Calendar.* London 1879–1902.

Scholes, Percy A. *Mirror of Music, 1844-1944, as Reflected in the Pages of the 'Musical Times'.* [London]: Novello & Co., 1947.
Scholes includes a brief chronicle of piracy and copyright problems noted in *The Times.*

Senelick, Lawrence, et al. *British Music-halls, 1840-1923; a Bibliography and Guide to Sources.* Hamden, Conn.: Archon Books, 1981.

A Short History of Cheap Music. London and New York: Novello, Ewer & Co., 1887.

Spark, William. *Musical Memories.* New ed., rev. and corr. London: W. Reeves [1896?].

Storey, Richard and Lionel Madden. *Primary Sources for Victorian Studies.* Chichester: Phillimore [1977].

Strong, Albert Ambrose. *Dramatic and Musical Law, being a Digest . . . with an Appendix containing the Acts of Parliament relating thereto . . . 3rd ed. London: 'The Era', 1910.*

Temperley, Nicholas, ed. Music in Britain; the Romantic Age, 1800–1914. London: Athlone Press [1981].
Separate chapters cited here under Krummel and Middleton.

Vann, J. Dan and Rosemary T. Van Arsdel. *Victorian Periodicals; a Guide to Research.* New York: Modern Language Association, 1978.

Victorian Studies: a Quarterly Journal. Bloomington, Ind.: Indiana Univ. Press, 1957– .

Weber, William. *Music and the Middle Class.* London: Croom Helm [c1975].

Wiener, Martin J. *English Culture and the Decline of the Industrial Spirit, 1850–1950.* Cambridge: Cambridge Univ. Press [1981].

Index

Most citations under rubrics in this Index are arranged chronologically, with the reference in the main being to the date (usually day, month, year) of the item. Exceptions to the chronological arrangement appear under Associations; Cases; Piracies; Pirates; Pricing; and Publishers, Music, where the arrangement is alphabetical.